Rich in Faith

Other titles by the same author

Great Revivals
Seven Pentecostal Pioneers
Seven Great Prayer Warriors

Rich in Faith

Increasing God's Gifts to Us

Colin Whittaker

Marshall Pickering

Marshall Morgan and Scott
Marshall Pickering
3 Beggarwood Lane, Basingstoke, Hants, RG23 7LP, UK

First published by Marshall Morgan and Scott Publications Ltd
Part of the Marshall Pickering Holdings Group
A subsidiary of the Zondervan Corporation

British Library CIP Data

Whittaker, Colin
Rich in faith: increasing God's gift to us.
1. Christian life 2. Faith
I. Title
248.4 BV4637

ISBN 0-551-01593-4

Text set in Times Roman by Brian Robinson, Buckingham
Printed in Great Britain by Guernsey Press Ltd, C.I.

Contents

Dedication to Isobel Ramsbottom, and the memory of Fred Ramsbottom and Maurice Hugo, three great missionaries from my home town of Haslingden, whose faith has inspired me from boyhood; and Douglas and Elsie Quy, whose ministry of faith has encouraged me greatly.

Introduction

Faith is for All

Faith is so simple – it is almost unbelievable. That is where the difficulty lies for most of us: we just can't believe that it is so easy. But it is childishly simple because Jesus himself said so. To make his point he actually took a little child and set him in the middle of his hulking disciples and told them: 'Except you be converted and become as little children you shall not enter into the kingdom of heaven' (Matthew 18:3).

All too often faith is made out to be mysterious and complicated. The very opposite is true. Again the impression is sometimes deliberately fostered that faith is reserved for an elite few. In truth it is for all – including women and children. In fact, they often excel when it comes to faith. Faith is a great leveller of people and that is one obvious reason God chose it. Our pride is usually the thing that stops us. It is a formidable barrier and why, in these days, the Lord is finding so many of his recruits for faith-exploits in the Third World. God's methods have not changed. His servant, James, is still trying to catch our ear: 'Hearken, my beloved brethren, Has not God chosen the poor of this world *rich in faith*, and heirs of the kingdom which he has promised to them that love him?' (2:5).

Reinhard Bonnke is an outstanding evangelist who is setting Africa ablaze with his 'Cape to Cairo Crusade'. Talk to him and he will tell you that people keep saying to him: 'Reinhard, you are an apostle.' To which he invariably replies: 'No, I am not an apostle, I know what I am, I am an evangelist.'

I must confess that is my kind of language. I am a pastor – just an ordinary, everyday, run of the mill pastor. After over thirty years in the ministry I know what I am and what I believe. You can't shepherd God's flock for so many years without being truly impregnated with the smell of sheep. Having had my life intimately bound up with 'the household of faith' I want to say I believe in people – ordinary people, everyday people, God's people. It is for these people that this book is written because I have seen so many of them become rich in faith while some so-called great people have died without so much as a millionth part of a grain of mustard seed of faith.

Returning on the London Underground to catch my main line train home, after a meeting with Edward England to discuss this book, some clever advertising by a big employment agency caught my eye. It said, 'Home Secretary? – No. City Secretaries? – Yes. We can't promise you a place in Parliament but as a foremost agency we can find you a good place in the City or in the West End.' While another proclaimed: 'Astronauts? – No. Down to earth appointments? – Yes'.

International evangelist with a ministry of signs and wonders? Probably not. But doing evangelism in your local church and seeing God work with you in amazing ways? – yes, a thousand times yes! Preaching to packed churches? Possibly not. But winning some to Christ, seeing definite answers to prayer, including the sick being healed and experiencing the supernatural leading of God in your life? – yes, ten thousand times yes.

Every born-again believer has the potential to become rich in faith just as much as in the days of the Acts of the Apostles. I was intrigued when I first discovered that the Acts of the Apostles has had several other titles down through the centuries, including 'Acts of the Risen Christ' and 'Acts of the Holy Ghost', but my favourite for the most apt title is: 'Acts of Apostolic People'. After chapter one most of the apostles do not get a look in; Peter and Paul almost hog the stage between them. The only way James can get another mention is by having his head removed by Herod. A pretty drastic measure, to say the least!

Ordinary people, however, litter the story like confetti round a church after a wedding. To start with, a hundred and seven such made up the numbers in the famous ten-day prayer meeting in chapter one. (You can hardly call Mary ordinary. So it was Mary, plus the twelve, plus one hundred and seven, which equals one hundred and twenty.) Three thousand ordinary folk swell the numbers in the second chapter, plus another five thousand by chapter four. By chapter six we have seven deacons but Stephen and Philip are soon in the signs and wonders business too. It is quite an ordinary kind of chap – Ananias, a Damascus disciple – that the Lord chooses in chapter nine to get the potentially greatest apostle seeing again and baptised in water and in the Spirit.

On it goes with married couples such as Aquila and Priscilla, tentmakers, getting dry preachers like Apollos, Spirit-filled; not to mention risking their necks to save Paul's life.

God clearly intended it to go on like that to the end of the age because Acts is the only unfinished (deliberately so) book in the Bible. The divine intention is for every generation to write its own Acts of Apostolic People, with vital supporting roles for all. I have met only a few, a very few, whom I have felt are truly apostles; but I am glad to say that my life has been filled with lots of apostolic people; the most wonderful people on earth – people of faith who do not know the meaning of the word 'impossible'.

My endeavour here is to give scriptural teaching on faith and demonstrate it in action from the lives of people of faith both great and small.

I have mapped out eleven specific ways to keep going on the road to faith-riches, starting where faith must always begin – with God himself. For what is faith but believing God? Not just believing about him, or that he exists, but believing him. The second stage examines saving-faith which always results in the greatest miracle of all – the new birth.

Christ is the Author and Finisher of our faith, and to become strong, faith must focus clearly on the Person of Christ, His full deity, His atoning death, and His Resurrection, Ascension, and Return. The third step therefore centres on Christ. One of the most hopeful signs of the revival of the church is the renewed interest in the Person and work of the Holy Spirit, and our fourth step takes us through some of the Spirit's riches. Faith is spiritual not mental, and flourishes only under the anointing of the Holy Spirit.

Step five takes us to the source-book of faith, the Word of God. This is where faith feeds and grows strong. Faith is an act and one of the ways faith exercises regularly and keeps fit is by giving, which is step six. Step seven sees us launching out into the deep for one of faith's most exciting activities – fishing for men.

When faith gets going, the Lord starts working in the realm of the miraculous, confirming the word with signs following and the Holy Spirit starts distributing his special gifts. That's why step number eight is a big one.

Faith has beautiful feet, but it also appreciates beautiful language, and the richer it grows the more of a language specialist it becomes – majoring on praise and thanksgiving, not to mention the tongues of men and of angels. Step number nine is set to the music of heaven.

Step number ten is the one we would all like to avoid because it is the unpleasant one of suffering. But the words of Christ must be faced. He is still saying: 'I counsel you to buy of me gold tried in the fire that you may be rich' (Revelation 3:18). The verse in Peter's first letter 'the trial of your faith, being much more precious than of gold that perisheth, though it be tried with fire, might be found unto praise and honour and glory at the appearing of Jesus Christ' (1:7), leaves us in no doubt that Jesus is talking about the gold of practical faith which knows how to get answers from God.

It is an interesting picture. Gold is the king of metals. It does not melt until it reaches 1063 degrees centigrade. The greater the heat the better the quality. Fire is the only way to refine gold, and suffering is the only way to produce the purest faith. God uses the fire of suffering to deepen and mature our faith. Modern goldsmiths do not know any new techniques and the twentieth century church is finding that there is no substitute for suffering. Wherever the church is moving in power, whether in China, Korea, Uganda, or Zaire, you will that the believers have endured the fires of persecution. It seems that this is the price that has to be paid by any who would be rich in faith and in this chapter we examine the question as to whether the church in the West is willing to face a time of suffering.

In a sense, the last and eleventh step is a never-ending one, for it takes us into faith's eternal dimension which will enable us to enjoy God's infinite greatness for ever as he unfolds age after faith-stretching age before our wondering gaze. World without end, Amen.

All the discoveries of modern man, his explorations in psychology, philosophy, and Eastern religions, have failed to throw up anything really new about faith. That is why the only text-book you need with this one is the Word of God and the only people mentioned in these pages are the Bible-believing kind.

All my ministry (apart from seven years as full-time editor of our denomination's weekly magazine) has been in pastoring. I have been the one, therefore, who has still been there when the healing evangelist has moved on. I know about facing the problem of those not healed. I know something about the agony of ministering to parents who believe in divine healing when the doctor tells them that their child has been born with a serious deformity. I also know something of the deep joy and satisfaction that comes from seeing a continuous miracle, which stretches over years, in the spiritual lives of such parents as well as a gradual physical miracle in the child and the thrill that comes from seeing such a child do one thing after another which the doctors said it would never be able to do

Thomas Myerscough of Preston was the great Bible teacher and man of faith who influenced such lives as W.F.P. Burton, the pioneer missionary to Belgian Congo, and George Jeffreys, the great evangelist and founder of the Elim Movement, to name but two of many. One of his favourite sayings was: 'He that has an experience is not at the mercy of him who has only an argument.'

It was when I was just a chubby little boy of seven years that I first met such a person. My mother was a dressmaker and she had opened a ladies' and children's outfitters in the main street of the little Lancashire cotton-mill town of Haslingden where I was born. One afternoon as I ran into the shop after school my mother stopped me in my tracks and said, 'Colin, I'm sure you would like to meet a real live missionary wouldn't you?' I suppose really I expected to see someone standing there in a pith helmet, with a Bible in one hand and a rifle in the other to shoot any lions that happened to be troubling the natives. Shades of Dr. Livingstone and all that. I knew enough to know that all the best missionaries came from Africa, that was where all the exciting adventures with crocodiles and slave traders took place – not dreary places like India and China.

All I could see was a small, rather thin lady standing there. I dutifully shook hands with Mrs Isobel Ramsbottom – shortly bound for Congo Belge – and went about my lawful business in the bread-bin in the kitchen before going out into the back garden to play cricket with my older brother. If I had but realised it, that apparently innocuous meeting changed the whole course of my life.

Unlikely as it seems with names like Fred and Isobel Ramsbottom, these were the first people to enter the Whittaker household who believed in miracles – not just in the Bible but now! Through them my mother started attending meetings where such people as Smith Wigglesworth spoke. A whole succession of missionaries trooped through our house in the years which followed and regaled us with stories of faith, about witch-doctors being converted, cannibals turned into preachers, miracles of healing, deliverances from dangers of all kinds, 'in answer to prayer'.

As I finish this book, the story of Fred and Isobel Ramsbottom has just been published by Marshalls under the title *African Plenty: A missionary life of miracles.* It includes the dramatic account of how Isobel was raised from the dead when the doctors had been unable to save her life. People with such experiences behind them are not at the mercy of those who have nothing more than arguments to offer.

It was not until I was in the ministry that I learned that when I was still a small boy, Smith Wigglesworth's daughter, Mrs. Alice Salter, had slept in my bed 'and claimed me as a missionary for Congo' as she later told me. Alice Salter was a real chip off the old Wigglesworth block, a mighty woman of faith and a great missionary. She was almost stone deaf but she could rouse a missionary meeting better than any other woman I have known, and better than most men too. Her husband, Jimmy Salter, was the co-pioneer with Willie Burton of the Congo Evangelistic Mission. Three times Jimmy had the sheet put over him for dead and three times God raised him up.

I thank God from the depths of my heart for the unspeakable privilege of having met such people when I was in the formative years of my life. I was fifteen when I first yielded my life to Christ in the Thomas Champness Methodist Memorial Hall, in Rochdale. The minister,

Rev. J. E. Eagles, M.C., was an old-time Methodist who preached the gospel with power and became Principal of Cliff College after the war. He it was who gave me my first chance to preach as a teenager on a Sunday afternoon in wartime in the Champness Hall. Due largely to the influence of people of faith like the Ramsbottoms, my text was: 'Jesus said unto them . . . Verily I say unto you, If you have faith as a grain of mustard seed, you shall say unto this mountain, Remove hence to yonder place; and it shall remove; and nothing shall be impossible unto you' (Matthew 17:20). It remains as my text.

Thomas Champness once said to Gipsy Smith, the world-famous evangelist, 'If God has a big contract on hand, faith gets the job.' God has a huge contract on hand – the evangelism of the world and revival in Britain. He is giving the job into the hands of people of faith. They count nothing as impossible. The Holy Spirit is giving them the tools of his supernatural gifts and they are going to finish the task.

Chapter One

Faith Starts Here

It is always important to start right. In this case as in everything else, the Bible is the best guide. It opens with the majestic words: 'In the beginning God created the heaven and the earth.' We must always begin here: first God. Beforc creation – the Creator. Before creatures – the Almighty. Faith always starts with God, which is good news because it means that wherever we are and whoever we are, we can start right now.

The Bible also happens to be a big book and so it is worth while remembering that concerning many of the great topics the Holy Spirit has gathered together the scattered fragments relating to a particular truth and given us an inspired précis. When it comes to the Resurrection, for example, then I Corinthians 15 sums it all up, while Corinthians 12 and 14 give us a concise guide on spiritual gifts, with the master class on love sandwiched in the middle in chapter 13. The greatest chapter on faith in the Bible is Hebrews eleven, and the writer gets down to basics when he says: He that cometh to God must believe that He is, and that He is a rewarder of them that diligently seek Him' (v.6).

A man who had become embittered over the death of his wife was teaching his daughter to write. He printed out the words 'God is no where', and instructed her to copy them. When she had finished she ran to show him her work. Due to her childish printing two of the letters were misplaced and he was startled when he found himself reading:

'God is now here'. It made a deep impression upon him and was a step towards the recovery of his faith.

God lives in the here and now and that is exactly what the writer to Hebrews is saying. We must believe not just that God exists, but the *He is!* According to the various polls the vast majority of people still say they believe in God, but for many of them it means no more than that there is a God somewhere, up there, out there – in the great beyond. However, something significant is happening all around the world and the difference today is not between those do not believe in God and those who do believe in the God, but between those who believe in God and those who believe in the living God.

Moses in his encounter with God at the burning bush in the desert came to realise this in a remarkable way. When he asked God for His name he was told: 'I AM THAT I AM' (Exodus 3:14). This is a fuller expression of the shorter form, 'I AM' or 'Jehovah' (YHWH). The indefinite tense used gives it the meaning equally of 'I was', 'I am being', and 'I will be'. Jehovah God is the eternal I AM. He is the unchanging one, completely unaffected by time. He lives in the eternal now. He is what He always will be and always has been.

Moses was then eighty years of age. For the first forty years of his life he was brought up in the royal household in Egypt and given the best education and training possible. He was very much the Prince Andrew of his day, daring, dashing and debonair. He was a prince commander in the great Egyptian army. He spent forty years learning to be somebody. Then his world collapsed around him when he killed an Egyptian soldier who was ill-treating an Israeli slave and he had to flee the country for his life. Disillusioned and disappointed he spent the next forty years keeping sheep in the Sinai desert. He was learning that he was nobody. But at the burning bush he met with the Living God and for the next forty years he learned what this God could do with a nobody.

Many people live in the past. They are always talking about the 'good old days', and in their view nothing is ever as good as it used to be. Others live in the future, spiritual Mr. Micawbers, always waiting for something to turn up. But people of faith live in the NOW because that is where God lives. Faith says you haven't missed it, neither do you have to wait for something that is always round the next corner, because faith deals in the present.

The greatest definition of faith to be found anywhere is given at the beginning of this famous chapter of Hebrews 11: 'Now faith is the substance of things hoped for, the evidence of things not seen.' 'Substance' here also carries the meaning of 'title-deed'. A title-deed is proof of ownership. If you have the title-deed for a property and it is in your name then that it legal proof that it is yours. You may not have actually seen the property but it is yours. Before you even see it you can say with confidence, 'It is mine'.

This is the language of faith. It is not make-belief but a believing which makes 'hope-so' into 'know-so'. John Buchan wittily defined an atheist as a man without any invisible means of support. Contrary to popular opinion, it is the invisible world which is real and the visible material world which is just a passing show. Living in the nuclear age this should not be difficult for us to grasp – all matter is just an arrangement of electrons, protons and neutrons and the world of the atom like that of the great cosmos is mainly just empty space.

The secret Moses learned at the burning bush and which sustained him for the rest of his life was that God alone is the great reality and 'by faith... he endured as seeing Him who is invisible' (Hebrews 11:27). 'By faith he passed through the Red Sea as by dry land' (v.29) but when the Egyptians tried to do it they were drowned. It is faith in the living God which makes the difference.

This was Paul's secret too. He said, 'We walk by faith not by sight' (2 Corinthians 5:7), and 'We look not at the things which are seen, but at the things which are not seen: for the things which are seen are temporal; but the things which are not seen are eternal' (4:18).

The next step is to be assured in your heart that God will bless you as you start reaching out to Him in faith. 'He is a rewarder of them that diligently seek Him' (Hebrews 11:6). That wonderful name Jehovah will repay further consideration. The various shades of meaning in the roots of the name combine to give us: 'the self-existent one who reveals Himself.' Jehovah-God is longing to reveal Himself to every one of us. We can be certain of this because God has gone to great lengths to emphasise that 'He is no respecter of persons' – in other words He treats everyone alike.

It took even Peter a long time to learn this lesson. Like most of us he was full of in-built prejudices as a result of his upbringing from which God had to prise him free. God had to repeat a special vision three times before Peter got the message. It happened in Joppa where Peter had actually been used of God to raise a notable Christian woman, Dorcas, from the dead. Coming as it did on top of the healing of a long-time paralytic man in the neighbouring town of Lydda, the whole area was experiencing revival with great numbers turning to Christ.

One day as he was spending some time in prayer, whilst the friends he was staying with were preparing lunch, he fell into a trance. In a vision he saw a great sheet let down from heaven full of all kinds of birds and animals none of which were 'kosher' to a strict Jew like himself. When he heard a voice telling him, 'Rise, Peter, kill and eat,' he refused point-blank even though he recognised that Christ was speaking and he retorted: 'Not so, Lord, for I have never eaten anything that is common or unclean' (Acts 10:14). Whereupon the Lord replied: 'What God hath cleansed that call thou not common.'

The vision was to prepare Peter to take the gospel to the Centurion Cornelius and other 'unclean Gentiles' further up the coast at Caesarea. When he arrived at the soldier's home he acknowledged his changed thinking by declaring openly: 'God has showed me that I should not call any man common or unclean.' After hearing Cornelius's amazing story about an angel appearing and telling him to send for Peter, the great apostle further stated: 'Of a truth I perceive that God is no respecter of persons: but in every nation he that feareth him and worketh rightousness is accepted with him' (vv 34,35).

This truth is so important that the Holy Spirit led James to emphasise it in his epistle also, stressing that it is inconsistent for one who professes faith in Christ to be prejudiced for or against people according to whether they are rich or poor, or to judge people according to their being well-dressed or poorly clothed (2:1). Throughout His Word God makes it clear that race or riches do not influence Him in His dealing with people, 'He is rich to all that call upon Him' (Romans 10:12). He treats us all the same. God has promised to bless anyone and everyone who believes. Contrary to popular belief, God has no favourites. Strangely most of us have a battle here: we find it easier to believe that God will bless someone else before we can bring ourselves to believe that He will bless us. However, the 'I am different' syndrome is simply inverted pride and must be dealt with ruthlessly. It is a stumbling-block to faith, a favourite blockage of unbelief.

Faith is simply taking God at His word. Or to put it another way, it is just 'believing God'. We are very fond of saying that God can do anything, but it is very important to remember there are some things which the Bible reveals He cannot do. For example our good friend James helps us once more by reminding us that 'God cannot be tempted with evil' (1:13). This brings us face to face with the essential nature of God – His utter and absolute perfect holiness. Evil has no attraction for the One true and living God. As long as we are in rebellion from Him, His holiness frightens us, but when we are reconciled to Him through the Cross of Christ, we find this truth warming our hearts not chilling them. We recognise that a Holy God is too good to do wrong and too wise to make a mistake. He is to be trusted utterly and entirely.

The Apostle Paul reminds us of another thing God cannot do: 'He cannot lie' (Titus 1:2). He is the God of truth. His every statement is to be accepted with fullest confidence. No wonder therefore that the writer to Hebrews exhorts us to 'hold fast the profession of our faith without wavering, for He is faithful that promised...' (10:23). We can safely put our trust in God because it has been revealed and proved that He is to be trusted and relied upon. He will not let us down or fail us.

A third heart-warming thing which God cannot do is mentioned by Paul in his letter to his young ministerial friend Timothy: 'God abideth faithful, He cannot deny himself' (Timothy 2:13). Our faith may fail – the strongest Christians have experienced their moments of doubt – but even 'if we believe not,' God's faith remains unshaken, unshakeable. That is why Jesus urged us to 'have faith in God' (Mark 11:22).

The Chinese have a saying: 'The journey of a thousand miles starts with the first step.' It is important to take the first step on the road to becoming rich in faith now. Unbelief asks sceptically, 'Where is God?' Faith responds: 'Where is he not?' The God of the Bible is revealed as omnipotent and omnipresent, in other words He is all-powerful, and all present. The Psalmist discovered that it was impossible to escape from the presence of God – no matter how early he got up in the morning or how late he went to bed God was always up before him and after him. God needs no sleep, and He never 'nods-off' – not even for a split second.

The psalmist found if he crossed the sea God was there waiting for him, or if he climbed the highest mountain he found he could not leave the Divine Presence behind (Psalm 139:7-12). God is always only a prayer away. 'He is not far from every one of us, for in Him, we live and move and have our being' (Acts 17:27, 28). He is equally the God of the infinitely great and the infintely small; He is not lost in the macrocosm of space, neither is He excluded from the microcosm of the atom. Nothing is too big for God and nothing too small. The vast star galaxies are under His control and the smallest virus cannot escape His attention. 'His centre is everywhere, His circumference nowhere.' The Lord God Omnipotent reigns and yet 'by the mercy of God, faith can break through into His Presence if the seeker believes the Word and presses on' (A.W. Tozer).

God is Spirit but that does not mean He is less real but more real. God through Spirit is a Person 'and can be known in increasing degrees of intimate acquaintance as we prepare our hearts for the wonder', says A.W. Tozer. The only thing God asks of us is faith. The Scriptures brand unbelief as the deadly sin because it shuts out God. Unbelief is faith in reverse. It limits the unlimited One, as for example did Israel in the wilderness and the Psalmist had to write: 'They limited the Holy One of Israel' (78:41).

It is not faith that is wonderful, nor we that are wonderful, but God who is wonderful. Faith must never focus on itself, nor on ourself, but only and always on God. He is the source of all blessing. 'Every good and perfect gift cometh down from the Father of lights, with whom is no variableness, neither shadow of turning' (James 1:18). Faith opens up our lives to God and enables Him to work in us and through us. God has revealed Himself in a progressive revelation which culminated in the coming of Christ. The more we know of God the more faith increases and the stronger it grows, realising that He is to be entirely relied upon, until it can declare with Job: 'Though He slay me yet will I trust Him' (13:15).

Faith's highest occupation is worshipping before His eternal throne. Faith gives all the glory to the all-perfect, all-glorious, all-wise, all-seeing, all-remembering, unchangeable, ever-living and ever-loving, sovereign and only God. Faith starts with God but it is the beginning of something which will never end – for eternity will be occupied with loving and worshipping the Lord Omnipotent.

We must believe God IS! There is no difference with Him, He is the Lord Who changes not. And we must believe that God will bless us as we come in simple trust to Him, because he is no respecter of persons.

Chapter 2

Saving Faith

Without love we are nothing. Without faith we can do nothing. But faith and love together are an invincible combination, they can not only move mountains – they can move the world.

It is saving faith which first locks the human soul into the love of God. It is obviously therefore of the utmost importance that we are sure about this basic aspect of faith. What is saving faith? 'It is heart-felt trust in God through the finished work of Christ on the cross resulting in the salvation of the soul.'

Archimedes said, 'Give me somewhere to stand, a lever long enough, and a fulcrum on which to rest it and I will move the earth.' The Rock of salvation is the place to stand, God's love is the lever of infinite length, the cross is the fulcrum and God has placed the end of the lever within reach of the hand of faith. Furthermore as soon as we put our hand on the lever we find His great hand closing over ours supplying us with all the strength that is needed. It is not our great faith which saves us but our little faith in a great Saviour.

It is not 'faith in faith', but faith in Christ. 'Faith is the tongue that begs pardon, the hand which receives it, and the eye which sees it; but it is not the price which buys it.' There is no merit in saving faith itself. To be exact, we are not saved by faith but by the grace of God through faith. In the words of Paul, 'By grace are you saved through faith…' Saving faith has nothing to boast about except

Christ and His Cross. The soul's first lesson in the school of faith is to realise our total dependence upon God himself.

A botanist searching in the Scottish Highlands discovered a rare plant he badly wanted but it was growing in an inaccessible spot half way down a cliff. He offered a good sum of money to anyone who would be lowered on a rope and get it for him.

One lad after taking a long hard look at the situation replied, 'I will, if you will send someone to bring my father and he holds the rope for me.' The boy's trust was in his father, not in the rope. He knew his father well enough to be sure that if his father was at the other end he would have checked the rope and the knots and everything else concerning his safety. Saving faith is relying upon God, it is putting all our confidence in God himself. God is our salvation.

The Passover brings out this truth very beautifully. A casual reading of the story may leave one with the impression that when God saw the blood of a newly slain lamb upon the doorways of the Israelite homes in Egypt, then He just passed them by and left them untouched. Nothing could be further from the truth.

A careful reading reveals that God promised when He saw the blood, He 'the Lord would pass over the door, and would not suffer the destroyer to come in unto their houses to smite them'. (Exodus 12:23: 'For the Lord will pass through to smite the Egyptians; and when he seeth the blood upon the lintel and on the two side posts, the Lord will pass over the door, and will not suffer the destroyer to come in unto your house to smite you'). The presence of Almighty God personally guarded every blood sprinkled home keeping out the destroying angel and the plague (v13). Jehovah Himself was their protector.

Not only was death kept out of their houses, but instead of the plague seizing the firstborn, life – the life of God – invaded the whole family as they sheltered under the blood and feasted upon the fire-roasted flesh of the lamb. They must have experienced a marvellous sense of the divine presence. The psalmist sings that 'He brought them forth also with silver and gold; and there was not one feeble person among their tribes' (105:37). The whole two to three million of them came out of Egypt wealthy and healthy. A moment under the over-shadowing of the Almighty was sufficient to renew the youth of the aged and infirm and set them up ready for the journey to Canaan.

Saving faith's entire focus is on God in Christ. It becomes strong by seeing the greatness of God and settled by realising something of the grace of God. God's grace is His love in action towards sinners. The Puritans often explained faith by the word 'recumbency', which is leaning upon a thing. It is the soul resting in Christ. It is absolute rest. The question of one's personal salvation is settled. We can never have faith to work for God until we have faith in God's work for us – namely His finished work of salvation at Calvary. The change comes when we realise that we are not fighting for victory but from victory.

Saving faith is heart faith, not just head faith. The heart in Scripture stands for the whole inner man – will, intellect, feeling and purpose. It means to believe with our whole being. Saving faith also includes repentance, and repentance is an awareness of the seriousness of sin. Under the enlightening influence of the Holy Spirit the soul is brought to the terrible realisation that sin is not just a pimple on the nose but terminal cancer of the soul. It is waking up to find that what you thought was just a common cold is a kind of spiritual AIDS – for which there is no human cure. The only help is in God and the only cure at the Cross. In the New Testament repentance and faith are not so much separate acts of the soul as one act looked at from the negative and positive aspects. Repentance is turning from sin to Christ, with the emphasis on the negative 'from sin'; faith is also turning from sin to Christ, with the emphasis on the positive 'to Christ'. Repentance is putting sin out of the heart; faith is taking Christ in. Or, if you like, repentance is turning one's back on sin; faith is turning one's face to Christ.

Saving faith is more than being forgiven. It is being justified, which is forgiveness plus. Forgiveness is the prodigal coming back home and having a bath to wash away all the filth and stench of the pig-sty, but though clean he is still naked. Justification is receiving the Father's gift of the best robe to cover his nakedness and fit him to take his proper place again in the household. It is Christ covering us with His own righteousness which gives us confidence to come into the presence of a holy God. Saving faith reverences and appreciates the power of the precious blood of Christ and rejoices in the love which would pay such a price to secure man's redemption.

Without saving faith we can never have the faith that enables us to be effective in our service for God and for the salvation and blessing of others. John Wesley is a classic example of this. For years he tried in vain to gain salvation by being very religious and doing good works. He fasted, prayed, read his Bible, visited the prisons, cared for the sick and poor, he even became a missionary to the Red Indians of North America with the hope that if he could not save their souls he would surely save his own by such a sacrifice. In a terrible storm en route to America he discovered to his horror that he was afraid to die.

On landing in Georgia a Moravian pastor got into conversation with him and asked him: 'Mr Wesley, do you know Jesus Christ? Do you know he has saved you?'

Wesley answered, 'I hope he has died to save me.'

The Moravian pressed him further: 'Do you know yourself?'

Wesley replied: 'I do' – but he admitted afterwards – 'I fear my words were vain.'

After two unsuccessful years in America he returned confessing: 'I went to America to convert the Indians; but oh, who shall convert me?'

Fortunately for Wesley back in England he met another Moravian, Peter Bohler, who showed him clearly the way of salvation by faith in Christ alone. Wesley still could not see it and felt he should stop preaching, but Bohler wisely advised him: 'Preach faith until you have it, and then because you have it you will preach it.'

The first person to whom he preached salvation by faith alone was a condemned prisoner under sentence of death. To his astonishment the prisoner believed the message and testified to having peace in his soul and went to the gallows with faith in Christ removing the fear of death. It astonished Wesley and led to his searching the Scriptures afresh.

He now believed that salvation was by faith and not works, but he was not ready to accept that it could happen in a moment of time. He wrote: 'I could not comprehend what Peter Bohler spoke of, an instantaneous work. I could not understand how this faith should be given in a moment: how a man could at once be thus turned from darkness to light, from sin and misery to righteousness and joy in the Holy Ghost. I searched the Scriptures again, touching this very thing, particularly the Acts of the Apostles. But to my utter astonishment, found scarce any instances there of other than instantaneous conversions.' However, he still tried to explain it away, saying that it may have been so once but not now.

Peter Bohler, however, was too good a fisher of men to let Wesley off the hook now and he confronted Wesley with several born-again believers who testified that God had 'given them in a moment of time, such a faith in the blood of His Son, as translated them out of darkness into light, out of sin and fear into holiness and happiness.'

Wesley acknowledged defeat, he stopped arguing and cried out: 'Lord, help Thou my unbelief!'

Within a short time that prayer was answered. In a small meeting of believers in Aldersgate Street, London, as someone was reading Luther's preface to Romans, it happened. Wesley said; 'About a quarter to nine, while he was reading Luther's description of the change which God works in the heart through faith in Christ, I felt my heart strangely warmed. I felt I did trust in Christ, Christ alone, for salvation: and an assurance was given me, that He had taken away my sins, even mine and saved me from the law of sin and death.'

That saving faith was the foundation of the successful years of service which followed. He had tapped into the infinite resources of God and his faith kept on increasing to the end of his long life. In common with Paul he preached 'the word of faith', that is, 'the word is near you, even in your mouth and in your heart' (Romans 10:8). Which more amazingly is the very message which Moses preached in his farewell message to Israel (Deuteronomy 30:14).

The context makes it clear that faith realises that we do not have to ascend up into heaven or descend into the depths. Faith always deals in the *here* as well as the *now*. Verse 8 is literally: 'The secret is very near you – in your heart, in your own mouth' (within your reach, within your grasp). Faith does not have to go on a pilgrimage to find its answers. God has placed everything 'within easy reach'.

As R.A. Torrey puts it: 'From beginning to end, at every step, salvation is by faith. God freely offers to us in Jesus Christ a manifold salvation; forgiveness, justification, eternal life, the right to be His sons, participation in His own nature, sanctification, heart-cleansing, an indwelling Christ, power to keep and to stand, and victory over the world and the evil one. We appropriate to ourselves every item in this salvation by faith. By grace are we saved through faith from first to last.'

As we conclude this chapter on saving faith, let it be emphasised again that there is nothing mysterious about faith – it is the very essence of simplicity. Faith is just believing God. God has made it simple; it is man who is always trying to make it difficult and complex. There is neither virtue nor merit in faith. Sir Robert Anderson expressed it perfectly when he said: 'In Scripture, faith is like healthy eyesight, unheeded and forgotten in the ease and enjoyment of its use. It is only in eye hospitals that people are always thinking about their eyes. Too many Christians are hypochondriacs respecting faith.'

Faith is not concerned with itself or about itself, but with Christ. Faith grows strong by concentrating its gaze on Christ.

Chapter Three

Faith in the Saviour

The lives of great people of faith may inspire us – but they may also depress us if we are left thinking that similar faith exploits are beyond us. The third step, therefore, is to realise that faith does not look at others, however great, but at Jesus – the greatest of them all. That is why the writer of the Hebrews epistle, after cataloguing some of the greatest men and women of faith, tells us not to look at these but to look at Jesus. The phrase 'Looking unto Jesus the author and finisher of our faith' (12:2) is literally: 'Looking off unto Jesus...' This is the only occasion in the New Testament where this word occurs and it emphasises the thought, 'Look away from these and instead concentrate your vision upon Jesus'.

When it comes to faith Jesus is way out in front of everyone, even Abraham, Moses, Joshua, David, Elijah and Elisha. The word 'author' used here also carries with it the idea of chief leader, or file-leader. Jesus is the leader of all leaders when it comes to treading the path of faith. As author and perfecter of faith he is the supreme example of faith in all its aspects. Before the incarnation, even before the creation, in eternity past, in that period which Scripture calls 'In the beginning' – was the Word and the Word was with God. There was God the Son with God the Father and God the Holy Spirit. Augustine said, 'Where love is there is trinity.' And one might add, where the Trinity is there is also faith, hope, and love. For these three abiding virtues are as eternal as God himself. There was never a time when the Son did not trust the Father. From eternity the Son was willing to implement the work of redemption even though he knew it would involve laying aside his glory and laying down his life in time on the cross. His earthly life is the final vindication of the principle of faith.

Becoming rich in faith is not a matter of hero worship but Jesus worship. Experience has taught us to beware of preachers who draw attention to themselves and not to Christ. Equally, where Christ is exalted and set forth in all his greatness, faith always feels at home and safe.

Harry Moorhouse was one of the most outstanding and successful evangelists of his day. It was his preaching on the love of God that revolutionised the ministry of D.L. Moody. But Harry Moorhouse knew his place as a servant of Christ. At a period when he had been experiencing the blessing of God to a remarkable degree in several places, suddenly in the next city the blessing was no longer there. He prayed much but to no effect. Then as he set out one day he saw a large poster proclaiming: 'Harry Moorhouse the most famous of all British Preachers'. He immediately insisted that it was removed and told the organising committee: 'No wonder the Holy Spirit is grieved, you have not magnified the Lord Jesus. He is the wonderful one, I am just a poor, simple servant preaching the glorious Gospel and saying, Behold the Lamb of God.

As long as faith concentrates on Christ it is safe. It was when Peter started squinting that he began to sink. As long as he had both eyes firmly fixed on Jesus he was able to walk on the water, but as soon as he allowed one eye to stray onto the waves he was in trouble (Matthew 14:30). Incidentally it is worth remembering that Peter must have had a second successful attempt at walking on water. As soon as he shouted in fear Jesus grabbed hold of him. How did Peter get back into the boat? I cannot think that Jesus carried him. Rather I imagine that Jesus said something like this: 'Now Peter, why did you start doubting? Let's try again, shall we? Just hold on to me.' And together they walked back to the boat. No wonder we read, 'And when they were come into the ship the wind ceased' (v 32). Such a happening left even the wind breathless with amazement, along with the rest of the disciples who could only wonder and worship.

It is clear from the incidents in the Acts of the Apostlesthat Peter had learned his lessons well in Christ's School of Faith. After the amazing healing of the life-long cripple who begged at the Temple gate in Jerusalem, Peter quickly diverted attention away from John and himself declaring: 'Why look you so earnestly on us, as though by our own power or holiness we had made this man to walk? The Prince of Life, Jesus, through faith in his name has made his man strong... Yes, the faith which is by him has given him this perfect soundness in the presence of you all' (Acts 3:12, 16).

Peter stands in stark contrast to Simon the Samaritan sorcerer who deliberately fostered the impression upon the people that 'himself was some great one' (Acts 8:9). When he tried to buy the power to impart the Spirit of God, Peter quickly put him in his place, exposing him as a deceiver who had no part in God's kingdom (v 21).

We have already seen in the previous chapter that salvation from beginning to end is by grace through faith. Salvation, however is not a system of wonderful teaching, it is God's scheme to provide a living Saviour who is wonderful. F.B. Meyer testified that it marked a new era in his life when he realised that God put everything our spirit needs into Jesus. He said, 'I do not talk about the cross so much as about Jesus who was crucified. I do not talk about the grave, but about Jesus who rose. I do not talk about the ascension, but about Jesus who ascended. He is with you and me always. It is not holiness, but Jesus the holy one. It is not meekness, it is Jesus the meek one. It is not purity, it is Jesus the pure one, Jesus, Jesus, Jesus! Not it, not an experience, not emotion, not faith, but Jesus. Do not think about your faith; think about Jesus, and you will have faith without knowing it.'

Faith flourishes in the presence of Jesus. Faith increases in proportion to our view of his greatness. That is why we are exhorted to 'consider him' (Hebrews 12:3). It is a great word for a great person. It is to compute. The greatness of the Lord Jesus Christ is a calculation beyond the scope of the most modern and sophisticated computer. It is an astronomer's word. The greatest minds after life-times spent scanning the wonder of Jesus the Bright and Morning Star have confessed that they have scarcely begun to measure his greatness. 'Through Christ', says Sidlow Baxter, 'the whole universe finds its originating and continuing expression. Therefore, not only is he prior to all things, he is *bigger* than all things.' It is also 'to reckon, to count the cost, to check a calculation, to calculate carefully.' Without the aid of the Holy Spirit we can never hope to make the vital calculation and faith will remain small and sterile. 'No man can say that Jesus is Lord but by the Holy Spirit' (1 Corinthians 12:3).

'Our one need is to know Jesus better,' said the saintly Andrew Murray. 'Consider Jesus! As God! As Man! In his sympathy! In his obedience! In his suffering! In his blood! In his glory on the throne; opening heaven; bringing you in to God! You must know Jesus better.' That is possible because God has sent the Holy Spirit for that very purpose, to reveal Jesus to every seeking heart. The great secret of ever increasing faith is a closer acquaintance with Jesus. He is the secret. Reject any system which belittles Jesus. And reject any teaching that makes it all complicated and difficult and only for the elite. Jesus is for all, and faith is for all.

Faith is not even in the book itself so much as in the Author Himself. In my love for the Bible I used to deeply resent it when people dared so much as to mention 'Bibliolatry' – I refused to accept that there was such a thing. As I make clear in a subsequent chapter, the Bible is indispensable for any who would be rich in faith.

Let me also stress that I believe absolutely that the Bible is the inspired Word of God, the infallible and all-sufficient rule for faith and practice.

Quite recently, however, the full force of the words of Jesus to the scribes and Pharisees hit me for the first time. They were spoken following his healing of the paralysed man on the Sabbath day. 'Search the scriptures; for in them you think you have eternal life: and they are they which testify of me. And you will not come to me that you might have life' (John 5:39, 40). Christ is in all the Scriptures and the Scriptures are all about Him. The Pharisees prided themselves on their knowledge of the Scriptures but when the subject of the book himself appeared they not only failed to recognise him but they crucified him. 'The letter killeth, but the spirit giveth life' (2 Corinthians 3:6).

That same attitude is still around today. Even the inspired Word of God, when approached in the spirit of intellectual pride and interpreted purely according to the natural mind (no matter how clever), ministers death instead of life and doubt not faith. Adolph Saphir, whom no one could ever accuse of not reverencing the Word of God, with penetrating insight says: 'By Bibliolatry I understand the tendency of separating, in the first place, the Book from the Person of Jesus Christ, and in the second, from the Holy Ghost, and of thus substituting the Book for Him who alone is the light and guide of the Church.'

It is now many years ago since I first read that time-honoured classic *Christ In All the Scriptures* by A.M. Hodgkin, but the thrill of discovering Jesus in every book in the Bible lives with me still. It transformed my study of the Word of God. Christ is the central theme of Scripture from Genesis to Revelation. As the Risen Christ walked with those two disciples on the Emmaus road his seven-mile long sermon was an unfolding 'in all the scriptures the things concerning himself' (Luke 24:27). 'All the lines of history and type, of Psalm and prophecy, converge towards one centre – Jesus Christ, and to one supreme event, His death on the Cross for our salvation.' When we see Jesus in every part of the Bible then our hearts also begin to burn within us and faith increases every time we see Him revealed in its pages.

In Genesis Christ is the seed of the woman who will bruise the serpent's head.
In Exodus He is the Passover Lamb.
In Leviticus Jesus is the High Priest.
In Numbers He is the Pillar of Cloud leading by day; the Pillar of Fire lighting the night.
In Deuteronomy He is the Prophet greater than Moses.
In Joshua He is the Captain of our Salvation.
In Judges He is the great Deliverer.
In Ruth He is the Kinsman-Redeemer.
In 1 and 2 Samuel He is the Faithful Prophet.
In Kings and Chronicles He is the Reigning King.
In Ezra He is the Faithful Scribe.
In Nehemiah He is the Restorer of God's City.
In Esther He is the over-ruling King with the golden sceptre of righteousness whose providence never fails in the hour or crisis.
In Job He is the Ever-Living Redeemer.
In Psalms He is our Caring Shepherd.
In Proverbs He is our Wisdom.
In Ecclesiastes He is the one to remember if we would understand life's mysteries.
In Song of Songs He is the Lover of my soul.
In Isaiah He is the Prince of Peace.
In Jeremiah He is the Righteous Branch.
In Lamentations He is the Weeping Saviour.
In Ezekiel He is the Man of Glory on the sapphire throne.
In Daniel He is the Ancient of Days.
In Hosea He is the Faithful Husband 'forever married to the backslider'.

In Joel He is the Baptiser with the Holy Spirit.
In Amos He is the Restoring One who accomplishes God's purposes for Jew and Gentile.
In Obadiah He is the Mighty to Save.
In Jonah He is the One whose rising after three days and three nights in the ocean depths is the supreme sign.
In Micah He is the Bethlehem-born Ruler.
In Nahum He is the Avenger of God's elect.
In Habakkuk He is the Justifier by faith.
In Zephaniah He is the Mighty Saviour in the midst of his people.
In Haggai He is the Rebuilder of God's House of greater glory.
In Zechariah He is the King, meek and lowly, riding upon an ass.
In Malachi He is the Sun of Righteousness risen with healing in His wings.
In Matthew He is the King of the Jews.
In Mark He is the Wonder-working Servant Son.
In Luke He is the Son of Man.
In John He is the Son of God.
In Acts He is the Ascended King who pours out His Spirit.
In Romans He is our Justifier.
In 1 Corinthians He is the Sustainer of His suffering servants.
In Galatians He is the Redeemer from the curse of the Law.
In Ephesians He is Head of His glorious Church.
In Philippians He is our Joy and Prize.
In Colossians He is the Pre-eminent One in whom all fulness dwells.
In 1 and 2 Thessalonians He is our Soon-Coming King.
In 1 and 2 Timothy He is our Mediator.
In Titus He is Our Blessed Hope.
In Philemon He is a Friend that sticketh closer than a brother.

In Hebrews He is our Heavenly High Priest ever interceding.
In James He is our Faithful Physician ('the prayer of faith shall save the sick...and the Lord shall raise him up').
In 1 and 2 Peter He is the Chief Shepherd and Bishop of our souls.
In 1, 2 and 3 John He is Perfect Love.
In Jude He is the Lord Returning with ten thousands of his saints.
In Revelation He is the Lamb upon the throne and King of Kings.

This has been the secret of all the great men and women of faith that I have known or learned about. Those who knew Smith Wigglesworth best of all testified that no matter where he started preaching from, his subject was always the same – it was Jesus. He did not preach healing, he preached Jesus the Healer. He did not preach the baptism in the Spirit, he preached Jesus the Baptiser with the Holy Ghost and fire. Jesus is the great secret of faith. It has been so right from the time of the Acts of the Apostles. When Philip went to Samaria and had a great revival with signs and wonders confirming his preaching, we find the secret was that 'he preached Christ unto them' (Acts 8:5). When he was witnessing to the Chancellor of the Exchequer of Ethopia it was the same theme: '...he began at the same scripture and preached unto him Jesus' (v 35).

Mr. and Mrs. Douglas and Clarice Scott exercised a truly apostolic ministry of church planting in France, Belgium, Switzerland, Belgium Congo (now Zaire) and Algiers for some forty years from the mid-1920's to the 1960's. Everywhere they went God confirmed their ministry with signs and wonders. Their ministry in France is acknowledged by the French leaders of Assemblies of God as a break-through in establishing the work in an extremely difficult country.

When they first heard the call of God in their lives they spent many months praying and fasting and seeking the face of God for a ministry of soul-winning and healing on the mission field. They initially went to France just to learn the language before proceeding to Africa to the Belgium Congo, but they started holding meetings in hired rooms and God began to bless so remarkably that they stayed on in France for many years. At the beginning before they had mastered the French language people came along for a good laugh at the expense of the Englishman who spoke such funny French. However, many who came to laugh stayed to pray when they saw what happened when he prayed for the sick. The news quickly spread and crowds increased.

But whenever any one was healed, the Scotts would never let the person go until they had asked them, 'Who healed you?' If the person gave any other answer than 'Jesus', they persisted with them until they got the answer they desired – Jesus. Throughout their long and amazing ministry this remained their unchanging attitude – they were very careful to give the Lord Jesus all the glory.

Apart from reports in the magazine *Redemption Tidings* very little was ever written nor is it likely to be. Douglas Scott died in the 1960's but his widow is still alive at the time of writing and in a Pentecostal Eventide Home in Bedford. However, she says very little about the mighty signs and wonders which God gave to them in so many countries, in all of which they left behind them churches which they had planted. She explains that it was part of their vow that they would not publicise what God had done through them lest the glory should be detracted from the Lord Jesus Christ, who alone is the wonder worker.

Nevertheless there is one miracle which has been repeated every week for many years. When she returns from the Sunday morning service she always sits down and plays the piano with great anointing and ability. The miracle is this – when she and her husband first went to

France they both played the violin. Mr Scott had been a jazz musician before his conversion. When they commenced their first little meetings in hired halls in France Mrs. Scott said, 'Well Douglas we must pray that the Lord will give me the ability to play the piano for the singing in the meetings.' The prayer was answered immediately; she found she was able to sit down and play all the hymns without any difficultly. And to this very day she says that whenever she sits down at the piano and wants to play a particular hymn she sees in her mind the key in which it is to be played and the music set out before her. Who did that? Only one could do such things – and His name is Jesus.

The last time C.H. Spurgeon preached in Exeter Hall, London, his text was 'Thou shalt call his name Jesus' (Matthew 1:21). He was not a well man at the time and in broken accents he gasped out as he finished his message: 'Let my name perish, but let Christ's name last for ever. Jesus. Crown Him Lord of all! You will not hear me say anything else. These are my last words in Exeter Hall for this time. Jesus, Jesus, Jesus. Crown Him Lord of all.' That is the only way to get rich in faith and to stay that way.

Chapter Four

Faith and the Holy Spirit

Faith and power and the Holy Spirit are inseparable. The wonderful thing to realise is that the Holy Spirit is longing to make us all rich in faith. In his Day of Pentecost sermon Peter made it clear that every born-again believer can be filled with the Spirit because 'the promise is to all... even as many as the Lord shall call' (Acts 23:38,39).

One of the thrilling happenings of the twentieth century has been the Church's rediscovery of the anointing the Holy Spirit. For centuries it seemed that the 'holy anointing oil of power for service' had been all but lost.

At the time of the coronation of Queen Elizabeth II in 1953 the church authorities discovered that they had literally 'lost the royal anointing oil'. The anointing oil used at the crowning of British monarchs is very special indeed, having been used and preserved over many years. After the coronation of the Queen's father, King George VI in 1937, the precious oil was returned to the Deanery of Westminster. But in World War II it was destroyed by enemy action during heavy bombing on London. The loss was kept secret but with the approach of the coronation of Queen Elizabeth it could be concealed no longer. It was a serious predicament. No-one knew the formula and the authorities were at a loss until a certain lady, hearing of the situation, disclosed that she had few drops of the anointing oil which had somehow come into her possession after the last coronation. A chemist was appointed to analyse it and compound a fresh supply. He even gave up smoking for four weeks before making it to ensure that he captured the full fragrance of the most special oil. At the great moment in the magnificent cermony the Archbishop was able to pour the annointing oil on the head and hands of the new sovereign. The assembled throng of dignitaries and loyal subjects shook the rafters of the ancient Abbey as they hailed her with their united cry of 'God save the Queen!'

In the last quarter of the previous century earnest believers of many denominations around the world set themselves to seek for the lost annointing oil of the Spirit. As they searched their Bibles and read church history afresh – especially the stories of the great revivals – they realised that there had always been some choice souls who had preserved the anointing and power of the Spirit of God in their lives. The enemy of souls had never succeeded in completely destroying the heavenly anointing oil. As these eager souls sought the face of God with fasting and prayer and dug deep into His Word, the Bible yielded up to them the precious formula as given by Peter on the Day of Pentecost.

What was that precious formula? One so profoundly simple that three thousand of Peter's hearers understood it on the spot and received what the one hundred and twenty close followers of Jesus (including the apostles and Mary and the other women) had received early in the morning of that great day. What was it? 'Repent and be baptised every one of you in the name of Jesus Christ for the remission of sins and you shall receive the gift of the Holy Ghost' (Acts 2:38).

How does one receive the gift of the Holy Spirit? In the same way that one receives the Saviour – by repenting, believing, and obeying. Christ is God's gift to the world, to sinners everywhere. 'Believe on the Lord Jesus Christ and you shall be saved.' The Holy Spirit is Christ's gift to His Church, to believers everywhere. The difficulty usually comes with the first word in the formula: 'Repent'. How often we turn that word into a harsh one, whereas in truth it is a gentle word, a broken one, a word of entreaty as well as of command. Brokenness is invariably a key to the blessing of God: self-emptying the prelude to divine filling. How many stories there are of people being marvellously baptised with the Holy Ghost and fire – just as soon as they were broken before God.

A man of God who was one of the trail-blazers of 'power evangelism' in the first half of this century was a gifted Congregational minister called Charles Price. (His name will be familiar to those who have read The Happiest People on Earth – the Demos Shakarian story, founder of the Full Gospel Businessmen's Fellowships. Price was the minister of God used in the amazing raising up of Shakarian's sister after a serious road accident – a stupendous and well-authenticated miracle.) He was born in Sheffield, England, studied law at university and was subsequently articled to a law firm in his native city before emigrating to Canada. After a difficult period without settled employment and in danger of making a real mess of his life, he moved to Spokane where he was wonderfully converted in the Life Line Gospel Mission. Very soon he was witnessing on the streets and shortly afterwards preached his first sermon. The way opened for him to enter the Methodist ministry; he married and moved to Seattle and pastored two Free Methodist churches in the area. Other moves followed, he was finally ordained in that church and then returned to Spokane.

Those were the days in the immediate aftermath of the Azusa Street Revival and the beginnings of the Pentecostal testimony. Two of his mission workers were filled with the Holy Spirit and testified to him and wanted to pray with him. He intended to meet them for prayer but in the interim he met a senior minister of his own denomination who 'warned him against becoming involved with such fanatics' and influenced Charles Price into modernism. As a result Charles Price stopped preaching the new birth and explained away all religious emotion from the standpoint of psychology.

He steadily climbed the ladder of success in Methodism because he was a clever man and a gifted speaker, but he was finding it too restrictive and he transferred his ministry to the 'broader field' of congregationalism. He became the pastor of the Congregational Church at Valdez, Alaska, and the superintendent in that part of the territory. Illness in his family compelled him reluctantly to leave the frozen north for the warmer climate of California where he pastored the First Congregational Church of Santa Rosa. Before long he accepted a call to the fashionable Calvary Church of Oakland. He was there during the period of World War I and he became a very popular social figure in the community, exercising a wide influence but not for the Gospel of salvation. His next move was to Lodi in Northern California where he packed the fashionable First Congregational Church with his popular preaching – but it was all just a social gospel.

When some of his congregation started enthusing to him about some great Divine Healing meetings in a huge tent – albeit over a hundred miles away in San Jose – he ridiculed them and decided to expose the whole thing. He advertised that he would preach next Sunday on 'Divine Healing Bubble Explodes' and then he travelled down to San Jose to gather his material for the great exposure. To his astonishment when he arrived he found that the minister backing the meetings was a friend of his, Dr. William K. Towner, a highly respected Baptist pastor. The tent holding six thousand was packed out with people standing around the outside. To cap it all, the missioner was the highly controversial woman evangelist, Aimee Semple McPherson, from Los Angeles. God used her to 'puncture his modernistic theology until it looked like a sieve' (to use his own words). The third night the only available seat he could find was on the front row on the platform near to his friend Dr. Towner. God was dealing with him and when the invitation was given for sinners to come to the 'altar' he was one of the first out – the glory of God so burst upon him that he ran up and down the main aisle of the tent shouting, 'I am saved.'

After the crusade he returned to San Jose to see his friend Dr. Towner and found that he was holding special meetings every night for those seeking to be filled with the Holy Ghost. Charles Price was now so hungry for God that he was there every night, in spite of the fact that 'the noise' put him off. Why couldn't people just pray quietly and with the dignity to which he was accustomed? And why oh why did some have to 'fall down under the power' as they termed it?

That particular night the church was filled to capacity and he found himself in the overflow meeting in the Sunday school room, which was also crowded out. He asked his friend Dr. Towner whether it was really necessary for people to be flattened out, full length, to receive the power of the Holy Spirit. Dr. Towner told him frankly, 'It's this way, Charlie, you don't *want to*, and therefore *you will have to*.' Already there were many people around the room in the prone position and Charles Price was still bothered at the thought of a Congregational minister such as himself being found in that undignified posture. When he spotted a little secluded place behind the piano he made for it, he felt quite secure when he found that there was room enough for him to kneel but not enough to allow him to fall over. He stayed there praying until after midnight when his friend Dr. Towner discovered him. After some more straight talk he persuaded Charles Price to move out into the centre of the room in open view. There all around him others were receiving the Holy Spirit, some of them were shaking and others had their hands raised.

Charles Price then told the Lord that he was willing for God to put him on his back in the middle of the steeet if that was necessary. For the first time he raised his hands as he prayed and he began to feel the power of God coming upon him. Suddenly he was prostrated under the power of God and as he lay flat out on the floor he started praising God. Wave after wave of God's power came upon him until he tried to say 'Glory' and found that he could not form the word but instead was speaking in other tongues.

When he returned to his church in Lodi he was a different man. He told them: 'Now you will hear one burning message from this pulpit – Jesus Christ and Him crucified.' To his astonishment over eighty people answered his altar call at the end of that morning. Very soon his church was in revival with over a thousand in the prayer meetings. Hundreds were baptised with the Holy Spirit and from 1922 Charles Price was launched on a ministry of evangelism and healing which took him across America and Canada and other countries of the world.

Signs and wonders followed his ministry everywhere. Vast crowds attended. Rev. Thomas J. McCrossan, a leading Presbyterian minister in Albany said that he had been through campaigns with Moody, Torrey, Gipsy Smith, Wilbur Chapman, and Billy Sunday but 'had never before found men and women under such tremendous conviction of sin as in Price's Albany campaign'. In Vancouver 250,000 went to hear him preach in the three weeks he was there. His ministry continued without any abatement until his death in his sixty-third year. In spite of his success he remained unspoiled, a humble servant of Christ. The turning point came when he was filled with the Holy Spirit, and the crucial moment was when he was willing to receive in whatever way God chose.

In the well-known Scofield Reference Bible, there is a strange omission in the footnotes on Acts chapter two. In his summary on the person, work and ministry of the Holy Spirit, under note number seven Dr. C.I. Scofield says: 'Christ indicates a threefold personal relationship of the Spirit to the believer: "with", "in", "upon" ' (John 14:17; Luke 24:29; Acts 1:8). He then proceeds to expound the first two, 'with' and 'in', but completely omits to say anything whatsoever about 'upon'. Unfortunately there is no doubt that the omission was not due to a slip by the printer but was done deliberately by Dr. Scofield because of his particular doctrinal stance.

Happily things are changing and more and more Christians of all denominations are rectifying the long neglected third relationship of the Spirit to the believer – 'upon' – the enduement of the Holy Spirit. On the vital issue as to the baptism of the Holy Spirit being a separate experience and subsequent to salvation, Dr. Martyn Lloyd-Jones spoke out with typical courage and forthrightness and compelled many to re-examine their position. As long ago as September 1964 he wrote in the Westminster Record: 'There is nothing, I am convinced, that so quenches the Spirit as the teaching which identified the baptism of the Holy Spirit with regeneration. But it is a very commonly held teaching today, indeed it has been the popular view for many years.' In his book *Joy Unspeakable* (Kingsway 1984) he says, 'But what is established beyond any doubt is that one can be a believer without being baptised by the Holy Ghost.'

How does one receive this experience? Thinking of Charles Price it means coming out of our cosy little corner behind the piano and surrendering our pride and our whole being entirely to God. Peter's second command on the Day of Pentecost was: 'Be baptised every one of you in the name of Jesus Christ for the remission of sins'. Baptism in water speaks of our identification with Christ's death on the cross for us. Being totally immersed under the water speaks of the death of our old life and its burial. Baptism is very much attending our own funeral. It is our public confession of faith that our past is not only dead but buried – finished with for ever. Coming up out of the water is our faith testimony that we are risen with Christ, new creatures, new men and women, born again and having the Spirit of Christ, his new nature. That is why for very many, baptism in water is a key to their being baptised in the Holy Spirit. It can be very costly indeed, for some more than others, if it conflicts with their traditions. It is total surrender to Christ.

The third step is receiving. As David Du Plessis was fond of saying: 'The baptism in the Holy Spirit is an encounter with Christ, the Baptiser with the Holy Spirit.' That takes a great deal of unnecessary mystery out of it. No Christian, no born-again child of God, is ever afraid of coming to Christ, or of yielding himself to Him. That is all He asks of us: that we come to him in simple child-like faith and surrender our whole being to Him – from head to toe, from the tips of our fingers to the tip of our tongue. And the last may be the hardest of all – for 'the tongue is an unruly member which no man can tame' (James 3:8). How fitting that on the Day of Pentecost the whole one hundred and twenty in the Upper Room demonstrated that the Holy Spirit was not only resident in them but president – controlling even their very tongues.

One receives the Holy Spirit by believing. Thousands upon thousands have received as they have acted upon the words of Christ when He said, ' "If any man thirst let him come unto me and drink. He that believeth on me, as the scripture hath said, out of his belly shall flow rivers of living water." (This spake he of the Spirit which they that believe on him should receive)' (John 7:37-39). If it is a scriptural experience you want then this is it. At Pentecost Peter declared, 'This is that which Joel foretold...' Jesus uses a figure of speech which we can all understand – drinking. Drinking here is believing. Believing is drinking, but it is drinking not just tasting, or sipping. Believing here is faith in an active sense not a passive one.

William Booth-Clibborn was the first of the famous Booth family to receive. In his Personal Testimony to Pentecost he tells how he entered into this experience way back in 1908. He says: 'So many never get anywhere with God because their faith is not active, but merely passive. They are not stirred to take hold of God. Such an attitude comes naturally to a broken and contrite heart overflowing with rejoicing as mine was the night I received. I got so that I could not stop praising God and the more I did the more I wanted to. As this continued my spirit was gradually shutting itself in with Christ, drawing nearer and nearer to Him until I was more or less less oblivious to where I was or what others were doing around me. I had no thought of speaking in tongues – who would dream of thinking about such things when the Lord Jesus Himself was standing there? But I realised my jaws were aching. It was not very long until something let go and I was singing in a wonderful language whose words I had never learnt, whose charm filled me with ravishing joy, and whose every sentence reached the Throne of God. I continued on my knees yet another hour intermittently singing and praising in this new wonderful tongue. The relish and ecstasy of that blessing has never left me.'

He also reveals something of the cost involved. 'My parents wished to go on with God in the light of His revealed truth; that is why in 1902 they resigned from the Salvation Army to which they had both devoted the best years of their prime. It had cost them something to part with a work that had grown to such proportions under their commands in France and Switzerland. We will not enter into the reasons why they left; they were plenty, and well defined as far as the more advanced truths are concerned. My parents wished the best to be obtained spiritually for their ten children, and God rewarded their faith by sending Pentecost to our family when we were free from all sectarian influence and independent of any organised Christianity.'

Personally, I do not believe that God has finished with denominations but I am persuaded that he has certainly finished with denominationalism and sectarianism. Only the Holy Spirit can make us rich in faith and the start of that walking in the Spirit is to be filled with the Spirit as they were on the Day of Pentecost. But that is only the beginning, not the end. Too many claim they were baptised with the Holy Spirit ten, or twenty, or thirty years ago, but show little evidence of being full of the Spirit now. One of the saddest things I know is a Pentecostal Church which is no longer moving in the flow of God's Spirit. Alas, I know of too many which are in that situation. On the other hand it is a tremendous thrill to be in a Pentecostal church which is moving on in the Spirit, which is open to all that God is doing today.

It has been my privilege to be a part of the Charismatic Leaders' Conference from its inception. To have fellowship with Spirit-filled leaders from almost every section of the Body of Christ is inspiring – and challenging. I am always conscious of the danger of being left behind by some of my Charismatic friends, many of whom are moving on in the things of the Spirit at a tremendous rate and experiencing God working with them, confirming his word with signs and wonders.

There can be no standing still in this life in the Spirit. Watchman Nee in a message 'The Tide of the Spirit' said: 'There is a principle to be noted. If you in your day and generation fully respond to God's requirements, you will find yourself borne onward in the stream of His purpose. If, however, you hold on to the past, wanting God to do as He has formerly done; wanting Him to repeat something that in your estimation ranks high in spiritual value, you will find yourself out of the main stream of His goings. To be a Luther in the sixteenth century was a good thing, but to be a Luther in the twentieth century would not meet the need. To be a Wesley was of great value to the Lord in the eighteenth century, but it would be inadequate in the twentieth. Unfortunately, many people fail to recognise the onward flow of the living stream all through the Church's history. You and I must be found at that point which the tide of the Spirit has reached today – not the stage it reached at some date in the past, nor the stage it will reach at some future date. The question today is not:

Will the tide of the Spirit flow on in this our generation? but: Will you and I be caught up in that tide? If we fail to meet the requirements of God's purpose for this present time, He will find others who will meet His need. Only if we have the authority of the Spirit shall we be found in the onward-flowing Spirit.'

It is a case of 'constantly being filled with the Spirit' as Paul says in Ephesians 5:18, where the verb is in the continuous present tense. To be rich in faith, therefore, one must not only have received the Spirit but daily one must be receiving of His fulness.

Chapter Five

Feed Your Faith

Dr R.A. Torrey was one of the greatest Bible teachers and soul-winners of his generation. His ministry spanned the globe and his books are still being reprinted. Early in his ministry he read a sermon by the famous evangelist, D. L. Moody, in which it was stressed that a person would never amount to anything if he did not have faith.

Torrey felt the truth of this and determined to have faith. He tried to work up faith and failed miserably. He confessed: 'The more I tried to work up faith, the less I had. But one day I ran across this text: 'Faith cometh by hearing and hearing by the Word of God' (Romans 10:17), and I had learned the great secret of faith, one of the greatest secrets I have ever learned. I commenced to feed my faith on the Word of God and as I have thus fed it, it has kept growing. If we are to have faith we must feed steadily, largely, daily upon the Word of God.'

We cannot produce faith by our will power, nor even by prayer alone – faith is a product of the Word of God. The man of the world says, seeing is believing; but God's man of the Word knows that 'hearing is believing'. Faith comes to us through eargate, not eyegate. 'Faith comes by hearing... and that by hearing the Word of God.' There was a period of time after the Reformaion when Catholics were compelled by law to attend Protestant services. Their answer was to turn up at church – but with cotton wool stuffed in their ears.

Today, listening is almost a forgotten art – we are

a nation of viewers. We don't turn up at church with cotton wool in our ears but nevertheless our ears are under such a daily barrage of noise that they are in danger of being desensitised. School teachers will tell you that, more and more, they have to raise their voice in the classroom because children in most homes live with a constant background of noise from radio and television. Consequently children tend to speak more loudly – even shout as a matter of course because they are accustomed to having to compete with electronic sounds of one sort and another. In turn, they tend not to listen unless someone is almost shouting at them! If we would become rich in faith it is essential to remove the cotton wool of unbelief from our ears and pray that God would restore to us the hearing ear.

Jesus often cried out: 'He that hath ears to hear let him hear' (Matthew 11:15;13;9,43; etc). He frequently stressed the importance of listening intently. 'Let these sayings sink down into your ears...' (Luke 9:44). 'Take heed what you hear...unto you that hear shall more be given' (Mark 4:24). And again: 'Take heed therefore how you hear...' (Luke 8:18). Reading the word really comes under this category of hearing rather than seeing, for whether the word is spoken or read, it is a matter of hearing with the inner ear; hearing and understanding; hearing and receiving the truth. The old adage still holds good: 'Read, mark, learn, and inwardly digest.'

Faith is much more a matter of the heart than the head. All too often our head gets in the way. It is not that faith is against reason, but it is rather that it transcends it. It is the acceptance that God's thoughts are higher than man's thoughts. Faith brings God into the situation. Faith is spiritual rather than intellectual. Faith honours God and God always honours faith.

When Aaron and his sons were consecrated to the Levitical priesthood, one of the offerings required was called the ram of consecration (Exodus 29:26). After this ram was slain Moses was told to take of the blood and 'put it upon the tip of the right ear of Aaron and his sons, and upon the thumb of their right hand, and upon the great toe of their right foot' (Exodus 29:20). Our hearing needs the cleansing of the precious blood of Christ if we are ever to begin hearing the voice of God clearly; as do our hands if we are to serve him effectively, and our feet if we are to walk in his ways.

Something very similar also was required when a leper was cleansed. The blood of the lamb of the trespass offering was put by the priest 'upon the tip of the right ear of him that is to be cleansed, and upon his right thumb, and right toe'. But interestingly in the case of the cleansed leper this is followed by the priest anointing the ear, thumb, and toe with oil. The oil upon the blood. Oil is a type of the Holy Spirit. In the words of Charles Wesley's famous hymn: 'The Spirit answers to the blood and tells me I am born of God,' – and this is always so: first the cleansing then the anointing.

What a difference when our hearing is cleansed, consecrated and anointed. The writer to Hebrews complained that many of those he was addressing were 'dull of hearing' (5:11). He had already reminded them of those who had failed to enter into Canaan because 'the word preached did not profit them, not being mixed with faith in them that heard it' (4:2), and warned them that unbelief would also exclude them from God's promised blessings.

The Word of God is unique, it reaches parts that other books cannot reach. It is 'quick and powerful, and sharper than any two-edged sword, piercing even to the dividing asunder of soul and spirit, and of the joints and marrow, and is a discerner of the thoughts and intents of the heart' (Hebrews 4:12). Faith stems from the spirit much more than from the soul. There is a very thin dividing line between what is merely soulish and what is truly spiritual. Soul and spirit are so closely entwined in our human personality that only 'the sword of the Spirit, which is the word of God' (Ephesians 6:17) can distinguish between the two. Under the anointing of the Spirit, the Word of God (whether read or preached) is like the wonderful laser beam which surgeons are now using to carry out the most delicate operations upon the eye. The Spirit alone can minister the word into our spirit, freeing it and releasing it into the realm where, like Paul we can say, 'I serve God with my spirit in the gospel of his Son' (Romans 1:9) – that is the realm in which faith really begins to operate.

That is why it is essential to read the Word prayerfully, always seeking the help of the Holy Spirit. Otherwise as Coleridge said, 'The Bible without the Holy Spirit is a sundial by moonlight.' I have yet to meet a man or woman who is full of faith who is not a person who regularly feeds and meditates upon the Word of God. It is their daily bread and, like Job, they regard it as more important than their breakfast. If it is a question of missing their Bible time or a meal, the Bible always has the priority (Job 23:12). People of faith also feed largely upon it – devouring not only whole chapters, but whole books.

Then when the Tempter comes with his 'ifs of doubt' they are ready to answer him as the Master did, with the Word of God, correctly quoted and in context: 'It is written, Man shall not live by bread alone, but by every word which proceedeth out of the mouth of God' (Matthew 4:4). It is significant that the first recorded utterance of Satan is one of questioning the Word of God: 'Hath God said...?' Which was quickly followed by his contradicting God's Word: 'You shall not surely die' (v 4). (Genesis 3:1,4). Whereas the first two recorded utterances of Jesus in the New Testament denote his willing submission to all God's requirements – even baptism in Jordan (Matthew 3:15), followed in His wilderness temptation by His resounding declaration of faith in God's word: 'It is written'.

This is also the attitude of all true prophets of God. Jeremiah, for example, when parts of the Scriptures which had been lost for many years were found in the temple, said, 'Thy words were found, and I did eat them; and thy word was unto me the joy and rejoicing of my heart: for I am called by thy name, O Lord God of hosts' (Jeremiah 15:16). David had the same attitude, as he reveals in Psalm 1: 'His delight is in the law of the Lord; and in his law doth he meditate day and night' (v 2).

Meditating is not sitting there with a blank mind in a semi-trance but 'chewing the cud' (which is one of the meanings of the word), prayerfully turning over and over in your mind what you have read. Like one of those contented cows grazing in rich pasture, after feeding on the grass it lies down and chews it over to extract all the goodness and digest it and turn it into rich creamy milk.

The Word of God also has a cleansing effect upon our minds. It is likened to water and, in Ephesians, Christ is revealed as 'sanctifying and cleansing the church with the washing of water by the word' (5:26). Every time Aaron and his priest sons wanted to enter the holy place in the tabernacle, they had first to wash their hands and feet at the large brazen laver (Exodus 30:18-20). They took this very seriously because God had said, 'When they go into the tabernacle of the congregation, they shall wash with water that they die not...' The laver was made from brass mirrors which the women had brought out of Egypt (Exodus 38:8), there being no glass mirrors in those times.

One of my boyhood memories is of a brass army mirror in my father's tin of shaving gear – this always fascinated me. With his permission (and sometimes without it) my brother and I would pull it out of its battered little case, polish it up and then gaze at ourselves in its brassy depths. My father had served as a signaller in the trenches in France and Belgium in World War I and we never tired of asking him to tell us how such a mirror had saved another soldier's life. It was in the breast pocket of the soldier's uniform when a bullet hit him but was stopped from penetrating his heart by the mirror. The mirror of God's

Word is a great life saver.

In the familiar story of Jesus washing the disciples' feet there is no doubt that Jesus based some of his vital teaching on this occasion on the brazen laver. The disciples would all of them have taken a bath before the Passover meal at which the incident occured. Salvation is a bath – it is 'the washing of regeneration' (Titus 3:5). Peter, after first refusing to let Jesus wash his feet, swung to the other extreme and asked Jesus to wash 'not my feet only, but also my hands and my head' (John 13:9). Using the background of the natural bath they had taken and their walk on the dusty streets of Jerusalem, Jesus explained that it was not necessary for Peter to have another bath after only walking down the street – all that was needed was to wash the dust off his feet. In the same way, spiritually, Peter had already taken a 'salvation' bath – all that was necessary was for his walk to be cleansed. As long as we are walking the dirty streets of this fallen world we shall need cleansing. However, we do not need another bath; we cannot be born again more than once, yet every believer constantly needs cleansing from life's inevitable defilements if we are to maintain our fellowship with Christ (John 13:7-10). Faith cannot flourish if we are distanced from the Christ by harbouring sin in our lives. But 'if we confess our sins he is faithful and just to forgive us our sins and to cleanse us from all unrighteousness' (1 John 1:9).

The Reformation is based upon the two principles: Christ only, Christ above all; and the Scriptures only, the Bible above all human authority. Adolph Saphir so rightly observes: 'The difficulties in understanding the Word are not intellectual but spiritual – in the heart, and conscience, and will. Hence the study of Scripture is based on self-denial.' The best book to read if we want to understand the Bible – is the Bible itself. The Reformers were right on target when they concluded that 'the Bible explains itself and, rightly used, it requires no higher interpreter. The

Bible is all-sufficient as a means of grace, having all needed power for converting the sinner and comforting his heart.'

Smith Wigglesworth, after his conversion, never read any other book than the Bible. He did not even read his own books, all of which were simply messages he preached and were transcribed by various people and published with his permission. He 'lived in the Book and the Book lived in him.' He breathed the Scriptures, they were his constant delight, and he believed them and acted upon them. That was his secret.

Which version should we use? Frankly, I do not think that it matters greatly which one so long as it is one of the many reliable ones which are available. As Saphir says, the difficulty in understanding lies in us more than in the Bible. The thing is, settle on a good version and then stick to it, along with perhaps the updated version of the Authorised Version if you decide on, say the New International Version as your daily reading companion. The very multiplicity of versions available can become a hindrance to faith unless we are careful. There is a danger of comparing different renderings until we come up with the one which suits our particular fancy.

Dr. W.E. Sangster, the great Methodist preacher, tells how one of the keenest Bible expositors he ever knew, unconsciously killed the habit of Bible reading in his church. 'A really able Greek scholar himself (and no mean Hebraist), his regular method in preaching was to take a text loosely translated in the English version and explain what it *really* meant. Month after month it went on. 'It *says* this: it *means* that.' The people gave up reading the Book. Can you wonder? Within their modest minds they said: 'It takes a specialised training to understand the Bible, and a specialised training which we do not possess.' So the genuine learning which should have made the Scriptures more inviting was unconsciously turned to this alien use.'

A little old lady who loved her Bible and read it constantly was one day given a present of a commentary by a well-meaning friend: 'This will help you understand the Bible' he said. After some time he asked her how she was getting on with it.

'Oh it surely is wonderful what light the Bible does shed on that book you have given me,' was her unexpected reply!

After nearly forty years in the ministry I have a great regard for many of the little old ladies I have been privileged to have in churches I have pastored. Anna of Jerusalem was a little old lady, a widow, but a prophetess and a giant of prayer who knew how to touch the throne of God. A person of the Spirit, like her compatriot Simeon, with him she recognised that the baby Jesus was the Lord's Christ and 'spoke of him to all that looked for redemption in Jerusalem' – whilst many, more learned but less spiritual, missed Him completely. Not a few little old ladies of my acquaintance have likewise been mighty in prayer and have believed for miracles and seen them.

It is good to know Greek and Hebrew and to be able to study the Bible in its original languages, but one has to be a very able scholar indeed before one is in a position to disagree and differ with the many gifted and devout andhumble translators who have given us translations which are so reliable and accurate, with no major doctrines or essential passages in serious question, as to enable one to say that the Bibles we have are 'the Word of God'.

Wigglesworth constantly affirmed that 'faith is an act' and it is. Faith without works is dead, being alone. Faith is believing God. It is not how much of the Word we know but how much we believe and are willing to act upon. We will never be rich in faith if we are afraid of stepping out on the Word of God. Like the priests who had to carry the Ark of God into the midst of the flooded River Jordan, we must be willing to get our feet wet if we want to see God work. It was only when they dipped their feet into the waters that God acted and cut off the waters and stopped the flow (Joshua 3:13 and 15). 'It came to pass... as the feet of the priests... were dipped in the brim of the water...that the waters were cut off...and the priests stood firm on dry ground in midst of Jordan, until all the people were over.' They had to continue to exercise faith all the time they stood in the middle of the river bed. It was only the invisible hand of God which was holding back the waters way up the river past the city of Adam. Faith is the evidence of things not seen. They had all the assurance they needed, the Faithful God had given His word and that was sufficient for them to stand on. Faith grows strong by constantly feeding on the Word of God.

Chapter Six

Faith to Give

God does not want us to have just enough – He is not like that. He wants us to have enough and to spare; that's the kind of God He is.

Thomas Champness was a great evangelist who founded the Joyful News Training Home out of which sprang that time-honoured Methodist centre of evangelism – Cliff College. Champness was a man of great faith and he ran his home very much on faith lines – but his idea of living by faith was very different to some who have left the impression that they were actually dying by it, usually in secondhand clothes and on a starvation diet. His training home was at Castleton, on the outskirts of Rochdale. One day he came into the dining room towards the end of a meal and found the bread plate empty. He immediately sent into the kitchen to have it replenished although the students told him that they had had enough to eat and were quite satisfied. He said, 'Never let it be said that the plates in this home were empty – there must always be something left at the end of a meal.' He was absolutely right.

No-one knew the heart of the Father like the Son of God. Jesus strongly remonstrated against the distorted image of the Father presented by the Pharisees and Scribes. On one occasion He said to them: 'You have not known my Father (whom you say is your God); but I know him and if I should say I know him not, I shall be a liar like unto you: but I know him, and keep his saying' (John 8:54,55). Jesus came into this world straight from

His Father's heart, and He came to put the record straight. He declared: 'No man knoweth the Father save the Son, and he to whomsoever the Son will reveal him' (Matthew 11:27). Reverently we may say that the picture Jesus gives of His Father is that He is all heart. God is love, and because He is love, He loves to give. He is (literally) the giving God (James 1:5), and He wants us to learn to trust Him for everything.

In what is widely acknowledged as the greatest short story in the world, the parable of the prodigal son, Jesus reveals the real heart of His Father. A devout rabbi acceded that this was one great new thing Jesus taught about God, that He loves sinners so much that He actually seeks them. One of the things which brought the starving prodigal to his senses was the remembrance that even the servants in his father's house 'had bread enough *and to spare*' (Luke 15:17), Champness was right, there are no empty plates where our Father God is reigning. In the dual miracles of the feeding of the five thousand and the four thousand, on both occasions all the people ate their fill and there were respectively twelve and seven baskets full left over.

Giving in God's way is a compulsory lesson for every believer who wants to become rich in faith. It is something every new convert should be taught immediately. It is practical and so very simple. All one has to do in the first lesson is to stretch out your right hand and then put it into your pocket or handbag and take out your purse or wallet. Count your money and give a tithe (one tenth) into the church offering. It is not that God needs our money, but we certainly need to learn how to give if we are to be His true children. God is neither mean nor poor, He is generous and rich. It is 'the god of this world' – the devil – who is mean and unkind and always libelling God. Do not believe a word the Tempter says – he is a liar, a cheat, and a deceiver. Listen to Jesus – He knows the Father best of all. I must confess I get annoyed when

I hear people (especially if they profess to be Christians) say after they have come back from a holiday in which they have enjoyed good weather: 'Well you know, the sun shines on the righteous . . .' What a misquote that is. What Jesus actually said was that 'the Father makes his sun to rise on the evil and on the good' (Matthew 5:45) – and if we really want to act as God's children and be perfect we must act in the same way.

We never lose by giving. God is no man's debtor. Jesus borrowed Peter's boat for a seaside pulpit but he returned it to him full of fish. He also borrowed an untamed donkey – but I have a feeling that when Jesus returned it the owner found that it was the most work-loving beast in his experience. It is impossible to outgive God.

Jesus said, 'Give, and it shall be given unto you; good measure, pressed down, and shaken together, and running over, shall men give into your bosom. For with the same measure that you mete withal it shall be measured to you again' (Luke 6:38).

Jesus was using a picture from everyday life in the market place. Here is a merchant selling corn. We ask the price and decide to have a bushel full. To our delight and surprise as Westerners, having filled the bushel measure he then proceeds to press it down unti he is able to top it up with several more generous handfuls. Next with a skill acquired over many years, he shakes the measure, taps the sides, until there is room for still more corn. He then tops it up once more, but instead of levelling it off he proceeds to heap it up until there is quite a pyramid of corn. You will find when you get home that you have got about another thirty percent for good meaure. Tithers and committed givers will all tell you the same story – they cannot afford not to give. They have found that God so blesses them through their giving that it literally pays them to give.

Thirty percent is very good return but Jesus does not stop there. After the rich young ruler had walked away from Jesus on finding the price of discipleship too high,

Peter asked: 'We have forsaken all and followed thee, what shall we have therefore?' In his reply Jesus made the staggering declaration that every one who has left anything for His name's sake will receive one hundred fold (Matthew 19:29). That is not one hundred percent, but one hundred times, or ten thousand percent.

Some of the extreme prosperity doctrines which have been going the rounds in recent years are to be avoided, but so also are many of the extremes at the other end of the pendulum which almost glorify poverty. Grinding poverty is certainly not of God. Wherever the Gospel of the grace of God has been faithfully preached it has always lifted people. Leaders of the Pentecostal movement in Mexico have testified that over the last thirty years or so they have seen people who have come to Christ lifted from the lowest depths of poverty to the place where many of their children are now at university and families are prospering. Yonggi Cho tells the same story in Korea. The faithful preaching of the gospel coupled with practising the teaching of Christ on giving has raised tens of thousands of his people from pauperdom to prosperity. Balance is important with every doctrine. As Spurgeon said, sound doctrine is very much a matter of walking a tightrope. We do not give to get, but we give because we love God and our neighbour and because it is right. Giving develops our faith.

Giving also helps us to keep things in perspective. Times of recession and unemployment remind us that God is faithful, and afford an opportunity to prove him. David had suffered adversity and could testify: 'The young lions do lack and suffer hunger: but they that seek the Lord shall not want any good thing' (Psalm 34:10). In his advancing years he could sing: 'I have been young and now am old; yet have I not seen the righteous forsaken, nor his seed begging bread.' In boom times we hold everything very loosely remembering that 'riches make to themselves wings and fly away' (Proverbs 23:5). God is the one great resource of people of faith. 'They do not trust in uncertain riches, but in the living God who gives us richly all things to enjoy' (Timothy 6:17).

There is an old story about a rabbi and a rich miser. The rich man wanted to know if the rabbi could tell him why he was so unhappy when he was so rich. The rabbi led him over to the window and asked him what he could see.

The miser saw children playing happily in the busy street, women shopping and standing around in little groups enjoying a bit of harmless gossip, and men going about their business. He said, 'Why, I see people everywhere, young and old, but they all seem to have friends and they look happy whereas I am lonely and miserable.'

The rabbi then led him across the room and stood him in front of a large full length mirror. 'Now what do you see?'

The greedy and selfish rich man found himself staring into his own sad face and replied: 'Why I see myself, of course.'

'Exactly,' said the rabbi. 'There is glass in both the window and the mirror, but when you put the silver behind the glass all you can see is yourself – and that, sir, is your trouble.'

When it comes to faith, Abraham 'is the father of us all', says Paul (Romans 4:16). It was when he gave his tithes to Melchizedek that Abraham learned the wonderful truth from him that 'God the most high is the possessor of heaven and earth' (Genesis 14:19). Consequently he refused to take even a shoelace from the king of Sodom lest he should claim he had made Abraham rich. It was after this that the 'word of the Lord came to Abraham in a vision, saying, Fear not Abraham: I am thy shield and thy exceeding great reward' (Genesis 15:1).

It seems certain that Abraham taught his son Isaac and his grandson Jacob to tithe. When Jacob left home to go to his uncle Laban he had nothing except his walking stick (Genesis 32:10). During the twenty years he was with Laban he had more than met his match. He was a bigger twister and cheat than Jacob – and that is saying something. Ten times his uncle changed his wages (it was a sliding scale alright – downwards). But Jacob kept his promise and tithed and in spite of everything that Laban did – Jacob prospered. At his parting Jacob declared: 'Except the God of my father, the God of Abraham, and the fear of Isaac, had been with me, surely you had sent me away empty' (Genesis 31:42). As it was he returned with a great household, flourishing flocks and herds, and, best of all, he found that the angelic hosts were watching over him (Genesis 32:1).

There was no shortage in Eden. God's plan was for man to 'Edenise the world' – make it one great paradise. Sin interrupted that plan. Jacob's twelve sons formed the nation of Israel and he wanted them to Edenise Canaan. They did to some extent but they never had enough faith to put into practice all that God told them. Some Christians have the impression that God is against holidays. Wherever they get that idea from I do not know – but certainly not from the Bible. The seven annual feasts provided family holidays throughout the year – finishing up with the whole family having a week's camping holiday at the feast of tabernacles, the keynote of which was joy. God is not a hard taskmaster, his commandments are not grevious. I am glad that sabbaticals are coming back into fashion. How wonderful to see churches with enough faith to release their pastors for a prolonged period after seven years. But God wanted the whole nation to have a year's holiday every seven years. Naturally they said, 'What shall we eat the seventh year? Behold we shall not sow, nor gather in our increase' God promised: 'I will command my blessing upon you in the sixth year and it shall bring forth fruit for three years. And you shall sow the eighth year, and eat yet of old fruit until the ninth year: until her fruits come in you shall eat of the old store' (Leviticus 25:20–22). If only they had had enough faith to do it – but it seems they never did.

God's plan today is for His holy nation, the church, to evangelise the world. Can it be done? I believe it can, but many leaders are wondering if God has given up on the affluent Western churches. It seems that He is now turning to the emerging churches in the so-called Third World. They are the poor of this world, but the rich in faith of this generation, and heirs of the kingdom, who are believing God can help them to evangelise the world. They are out-giving us and out-believing us.

I shall always thank God for those believers who first taught me the blessing of tithing and not stopping there but honouring God with the first-fruits of every increase and giving as much as possible – especially for missions and evangelism. Through thirty-seven years of happy married life, all of them in the ministry, my wife Hazel and I have proved God. With two sets of twins to bring up on what for many years was indeed a pastoral pittance, nevertheless my precious wife has never once jibbed about putting aside God's portion first. I think that without exception every time God has called us to move we have always taken a drop in salary – but by the time we have left a church, we have always been better off and so has every church we have pastored. God is faithful.

I remember when I first launched out into full-time service for God and a former school friend, a non-Christian, asked me about pay and conditions and I told him that there was no guaranteed salary, it was all a matter of trusting God. He was dismayed for me but God has never failed us. It has not been easy and after all these years in the ministry, it still is not. More and more churches are waking up to faith-promise giving and other exciting and challenging aspects of stewardship, but too many are fast asleep. Far too many still think that missionaries and ministers should not be paid a generous salary. I say this only to make sure that no-one gets a wrong impression and thinks that if you tithe, God will automatically prosper you and make life easy. God always gives us chance to exercise our faith.

Remember the second law of harvest. The first is the familiar one: 'We reap what we sow'. But the second is equally true – and being a law it is sure and certain and always works. It is found in 2 Corinthians 9:6-8.'we reap how we sow.' 'Sow sparingly...then reap sparingly; sow bountifully – and you will reap bountifully.' The more you give the more you will get. But never give grudgingly for God loves a cheerful giver, and never give with an ulterior motive for God searches the heart. We can never deceive Him.

All believers are called to give; it is a weekly act of faith. 'Upon the first day of the week, let every one of you lay by him in store, as God has prospered him...' (2 Corinthians 16:2). One pastor of my acquaintance, who is always moving ahead in faith, said recently, 'Don't give from what you get, but from what you believe God wants you to have.' He was doing that himself and I am sure he will get it. You always get what you can truly believe for.

Some, however, are called to a special ministry of giving. Giving is their main ministry. Paul makes this clear in his intriguing list of ministries in Romans 12. After mentioning the usual ones of prophecy, teaching, exhortation, and saying those with such gifts must 'wait on their ministering,' he then surprises us by inserting: 'He that giveth, let him do it with simplicity' (v 8).

Over the years there have been many notable instances of Christian businessmen who have realised that God has prospered them so that they may be His faithful stewards. When God finds people He can trust with wealth He will bless them accordingly. 'Remember the Lord thy God: for it is he that giveth thee power to get wealth' said Moses (Deuteronony 8:18). Dig back a little and it is amazing to discover how many world-famous businesses were started by believers who honoured God in their giving and took Him into partnership with them: names such as

Heinz (the 57 Varieties man), and Colgate (soap and toothpaste).

William Colgate left home as a boy and headed for New York because his family was so poor. On the way he met a Christian friend, a canal-boat captain, who prayed with him when he discovered where William was going. When they got up from their knees the Captain asked William what he could do. 'Make tallow candles and soft soap,' he answered. 'Well then,' said his friend, 'give your heart to God and ten cents out of every dollar you earn and maybe God will make you a great soap maker one day.' Young Colgate did just that. As he prospered he upped his giving to fifteen percent, then twenty-five percent, until finally he was giving half of his income to God's work and world missions.

When faith is controlling our giving, it is not a question of 'giving until it hurts' – but of 'giving because it only hurts when we are not able to give.' How glad we are that Luke and Paul rescued the ninth beatitude of Jesus for us: 'It is more blessed to give than to receive' (Acts 20:35). If Paul had not quoted it and Luke reported it, we would not have had it. It was so important that it was almost the last thing Paul said to his Ephesian friends in his farewell: 'Remember these words of the Lord Jesus,' he counselled them.

Never forget them and always practice them if you would become rich in faith.

Chapter Seven

Soul-Winning Faith

'Compared with evangelism everything else that happens in the Church is like re-arranging the furniture when the house is on fire,' said the late David Watson.

When Catherine Booth lay dying she was visited by her daughter, the Marechale, and she told her: 'When one comes to the end of life's road, one discovers afresh that there is only one thing worth living for and that is winning souls for Jesus.'

The Word of God reminds us: 'He that winneth souls is wise' (Proverbs 11:30). The person who concentrates on soul-winning is wise indeed because it is the only investment that will last forever and which we shall be able to see forever. Diamonds are not for ever – souls are. That is why we find Paul telling his Thessalonian converts: 'What is our hope, or joy, or crown of rejoicing? Are not even you in the presence of our Lord Jesus Christ at his coming? For you are our glory and joy' (1 Thessalonians 2:19,20). In that day when Christ comes and we stand in His presence, if there is just one soul that we have been instrumental in bringing to Christ, then (in the words of a great Scottish preacher) 'our heaven will be two heavens'.

'Possibility thinking' is a wonderful phrase which people of faith have added to their vocabulary in recent years. Indulge in a little bit of possibility thinking right now. If you have never had the joy of winning one soul begin now to believe for your first soul. If you have been used of God to win some souls to Christ then begin to believe now for

God to double your catch. Believe me – no. Believe Him who said: 'Follow me and I will make you fishers of men' (Matthew 4:19). This is a wonderful promise. Look at it carefully: 'I will make you...' He promises that *He* will do the making and all He asks is that we follow Him.

On Sunday morning, 4th May 1986, I felt a strong leading to warn our congregation at the Mount of Olives, Bristol, that unless many of them stirred themselves they would be left behind by new converts that God would bring into our midst, who, within a few months of being saved, would be winning souls and surpassing them in the gifts of the Spirit. We then proceeded with our usual time of praise and worship leading up to communion.

Suddenly there was quite a disturbance and I opened my eyes to see the cause. Some sixteen or eighteen people – four or five families with their children – had come in. (Afterwards we learned they were late because they had not known the time our service commenced). It was soon obvious that they loved the Lord from the way they entered vigorously and joyously into our worship. Afterwards I discovered that they were 'Travellers' or 'Gypsies' who, in the week, had attended our National Conference Celebration and Bible Week at Minehead. Some of them had actually been converted that very week after being taken to the Minehead Celebration by gypsy friends, who themselves were just new converts. One of the gypsy leaders was so anxious for the new converts to be baptised by immersion before they dispersed throughout the country for their usual summer itineraries that he wanted me to arrange a baptismal service that very evening. We finally settled for the following week on the Sunday evening.

None of our congregation will ever forget it – there were eighteen candidates in all, twelve gypsies and six of our own. I shared the service and baptisms with one of the gypsy evangelists. What beautiful liberty and freedom of praise we experienced. Our gypsy friends danced for joy as each convert testified of the change Christ had made in their lives. Never before had I experienced such a dramatic and almost instant fulfilment of a prophetic word as that given me on the previous Sunday morning. After that baptismal service we did not see any of them again until those returned who have their winter quarters in the Bristol area. They thrilled us and humbled us as they told how in their travels they had witnessed boldly for Christ and had had the joy of winning thirty-one people to Christ.

Having been privileged to attend the first British Gypsy Convention on a farm at Ilkeston, Derbyshire, over the weekend of 30th and 31st July 1983, I was not entirely surprised at the way God is using them – it is their day of visitation. There were only about two hundred at that first convention, including French gypsies who had come over with Clement le Cossec, the leader of the International Gypsy Movement.

Only those who looked with the eyes of faith could see any prospects for a move of God among British gypsies. For several years before 1983 a number of unsuccessful attempts had been made to commence a British work. To be honest, the atmosphere at the first convention was more like a fairground than a convention. There were nearly sixty trailers on the field and the majority of those present were unconverted. The Baptismal service on the Sunday morning in the tent was both moving and hilarious. Make no mistake, the gypsy evangelists were in deadly earnest, but the sight of them trying to immerse men of sixteen and seventeen stone in weight in a kiddy's paddling pool was accomplished only with difficulty. It required some strange antics to get some of the larger ones 'right under' but not one escaped without being totally immersed. The only sprinkling was reserved for the more than enthusiastic congregation, few of whom escaped as the robust candidates emerged from the pool. Nevertheless, fifteen gypsies professed salvation, twenty recent converts were baptised and several were filled with the Holy Spirit.

Four years later there are around two thousand Christian gypsies in Britain and their number is increasing all the time. In France and Spain there are many times that number.

The revival among the gypsies started in France at Lisieux, Normandy in 1950. A gypsy woman, Mme Duvil-Reinhardt, was given a Christian tract which she kept in her handbag. Some months later her son, Zino, was taken to the local hospital where the doctors operated on him for tubercular peritonitis, but the surgeon informed his mother that there was no hope. She was distracted at the news and did not know where to turn. Then she thought of the tract which had spoken of divine healing. With the help of a woman in a shop she found the address of a Pentecostal preacher. She said: 'I entered the Pentecostal church and interrupted the preacher. I told him: "Sir, my son is dying. Come and pray for him." He answered: "No, your son will not die, because God is all powerful and able to deliver him." Then the preacher, Pastor Gichtenaere, went to the hospital to see him and to lay hands on him in the name of the Lord. Several days later my son left the hospital completely cured. Then I and my family surrendered completely to Jesus.'

The mother then sent a letter to another son, Mandz, who travelled some two hundred miles to see her and his brother, and was also converted. Mandz was destined to become the first gypsy preacher of the movement. Along with other gypsies they attended the services in Lisieux and in the providence of God, Pastor Clement le Cossec made their acquaintance. Le Cossec was God's man to lead the gypsy revival.

The gypsies left Lisieux and resumed their usual travels. It was two years later before Le Cossec met up with them again in Brest, Brittany. He found that they were still going on with Christ but were meeting up with difficulties. Because they were not 'legally' married, ministers would not baptise them. Le Cossec was shocked and touched at their predicament and took immediate steps to get their marriages formalised and to baptise them by immersion. From then on Le Cossec committed himself to helping the gypsies. Six years later there were three thousand gypsy converts, all of them baptised. In the beginning about ninety-five percent of the new converts were illiterate so Le Cossec conducted classes on the Bible and taught reading and writing. Le Cossec is currently president of the Worldwide Evangelical Gypsy Mission which has work in thirty-four countries with around a quarter of a million Christian gypsies. There are more than thirty thousand in France and some of their gypsy conventions attract crowds of tens of thousands. After a fairly slow start the work is now growing at a tremendous rate.

Clement Le Cossec's great talent lies in training others to be soul-winning preachers. Although he is the leader of such a great movement he is totally unspoiled. He treats everyone he meets – even children – as equals and adults. He never treats people as children. He is a great encourager of people, always showing more faith in their capabilities than they themselves have.

In 1975 he was in England and met a group of unconverted Irish gypsies. They were poor, ragged, boisterous and given to heavy drinking. Instead of railing at them he started by saying: 'Unless some of you become preachers, too, your people will not hear the good news.' He did not tell them how wicked they were compared with the preachers; rather he held out the prospect before them of being colleagues, he showed them a vision of their lives transformed by Christ.

God's methods are men – and women. Wherever God can find people with faith He is pleased to bless and use them, especially in seeking the lost. When it comes to soul-winning it is not that we do not know enough but that we do not GO enough. The biggest word in evangelism is spelt G O!

There are three instructive incidents in the life

of Peter which show us how Christ was preparing him to be a fisher of men. The first occurred after Jesus had used Peter's boat for a pulpit to preach to a great crowd on the shore. Poor Peter, he must have been exhausted – he and his partners had fished all night and had not caught even a tiddler. Nevertheless, as a good fisherman, he fought against sleep and the inevitable discouragement of a fruitless night and got down to the dull but necessary routine of washing his net. He obviously did not mind Jesus borrowing his boat but for Jesus then to tell him to pull out again into the deep waters for another attempt to catch fish was ridiculous – and Peter as good as told Him so. After all, Jesus was a carpenter so what did he know about fishing? He soon found out!

Wearily Peter and Andrew bent their backs to the oars and, with resentment building up inside him at every stroke, Peter soon decided they had gone far enough. They were still within hailing distance of the shore and Peter knew only too well that many of his friends would be laughing at him. Every fisherman knew it was the wrong time to catch fish. Carelessly he let the net down into the waters. He looked at Jesus and for a moment their eyes met: Peter sensed that Jesus knew exactly what he was thinking. Then it happened – suddenly it seemed that every fish in Galilee was fighting to get into Peter's net. In all his experience he had never seen anything like it. There were so many his net began to break. Peter shouted to his partners, James and John, to come and help. They did not need a second invitation. Even from the shore they could see the excited flashes of silver in the bright morning sunlight as the fish leapt out of the water. Within minutes they were alongside Peter and soon their net too was filled to breaking point. They piled both boats so high with fish that they began to sink. It was a miracle and as a fisherman Peter recognised and appreciated it more than any mere land-lubber. He was ashamed to look Jesus in the face. Turning water into wine was wonderful but so far as

Peter was concerned it was nothing compared to this. He knew fish and how hard it was to catch them. Jesus had most convincingly demonstrated his power over nature.

Peter was so convicted of his unbelief and his wrong attitude to Jesus that he fell on his knees before him and confessed: 'Depart from me; for I am a sinful man, O Lord.' To his amazement and relief Jesus instead of being angry with him simply said, 'Fear not; from henceforth thou shalt catch men.' Peter's tiredness vanished. He was being called to fish for the biggest catch of all – men.

That story could well be called 'The failure of the Experts' – for the best fishermen on Galilee had toiled all night and caught nothing. The first lesson Jesus was teaching them about soul-winning was that without Him they could do nothing. Winning souls is a supernatural business. Without Christ all our expertise amounts to nothing. But with Christ 'we can do all things' (Philippians 4:13) – providing we are willing to obey Him. With Peter we will often find that the opportunity for a big catch comes when we are tired out. It is not by chance that Paul slips 'weariness' into his impressive list of sufferings for Christ (2 Corinthians 11:27).

Jesus repeatedly broke through the weariness barrier in his mission to seek and to save that which was lost. At Jacob's well, though weary, hungry and thirsty, he was ready to talk to a promiscuous Samaritan woman (John 4:6,31). Having won her, he then fasted and prayed for her as she returned home to the city to witness. This was the secret behind the success of her witnessing. Faith sees 'the fields white, already to harvest' and oceans teeming with fish just waiting to be caught. Through his broken net Peter learned the hard way that when Jesus said 'let down your nets' (plural) it was not enough only to 'let down the net' (singular) (Luke 5:4,5). God can save three thousand or five thousand at once. Faith believes in mass evangelism.

The second incident in Jesus' tuition of Peter occurred when he sent Peter to fish for their taxes (Matthew

17:24-27). Imagine how Peter must have felt when Jesus told him: 'Go to the sea and cast an hook and take up the first fish that comes up, and when you have opened his mouth, you shall find a piece of money: that take and give unto them (the collectors of the tax) for me and you.' Peter probably had not used a line and hook since he was a boy! No doubt he felt more than a little foolish as he set out on his unique fishing expedition, hoping against hope that he would not bump into any of his fishing colleagues on the way.

But he knew Jesus well enough now to know that 'he was the one who must be obeyed'. He did not have long to wait for his catch. The one fish out of tens of thousands in blue Galilee with a silver coin in its mouth was homing in on Peter's hook as fast as it could swim. Its Creator had called for it to come. With fumbling excited fingers Peter unhooked it and opened its mouth – and his faith soared as he held the miracle coin in his hand. He was learning that Jesus had power over all fish; it was the prelude to his learning that Jesus the Christ of God 'had power over all flesh' and was able to 'give them eternal life' (John 17:2).

The Lord knows all about men – He knows 'what is in man' (John 2:25). He knows the position and spiritual state of every person in the world and as we learn to be sensitive to the Holy Spirit, He will lead us to the right person at the right time. Timing is all important in life. It is timing which distinguishes the true professional whether in cricket, soccer, or any sport, or in acting. If you object to that word professional, it is instructive to learn that when Jesus called Peter to be a fisher of men he used the word which denotes one who fishes for a business, not a part-time fisherman who fishes for sport. Real people of faith are always willing to learn – even by their mistakes. John Wimber is so right when he says that faith is spelt R-I-S-K. One of the constant risks is that of making a fool of yourself – and most of us find that too big a risk because it might injure our pride. Soul-winning involves a daily taking up of one's cross.

Philip had to leave a revival in Samaria to go into the desert to speak to one soul. But that one was a big fish – with a key not a coin in its mouth. The Lord knew that this man – the Chancellor of the Exchequer to Queen Candace of Ethiopia – was the key to a whole country. As always God's timing was perfect. Philip received explicit instructions from the angel of the Lord. He was to head south for the Jerusalem – Gaza desert highway. He was on foot and the Chancellor was travelling at a much faster speed in his splendid chariot from another direction but their two paths coincided perfectly. Being chauffeur-driven he was able as he travelled to read the copy of Isaiah he had bought in Jerusalem. Suddenly the Spirit of God spoke to Philip and told him: 'Go near and join yourself to this chariot' (Acts 8:29). Even though God had engineered the meeting perfectly Philip still had to run or he would have missed the opportunity. The Greeks rightly pictured opportunity as a swift runner with a lock of hair at the front but bald behind – you had to catch him as he came – once past it was too late!

As Philip ran he heard the well-dressed rich man in the Rolls Royce of a chariot reading aloud from Isaiah chapter 53 and his heart leapt for joy. He had not mistaken God's leading. Boldly he called out: 'Do you understand what you are reading?' The Ethiopian had been longing for somebody to guide him through this difficult book and he immediately invited the weary and dusty Philip to join him in his chariot. It was no coincidence that he was right in the middle of the greatest prophetic picture of the vicarious sufferings of Christ in the Scriptures. 'Philip opened his mouth and began at the same scripture and preached unto him Jesus.' Very soon the Chancellor was ready to confess Christ: 'I believe that Jesus Christ is the Son of God,' he declared, and at the next oasis Philip duly baptised him. When the Chancellor returned home it is reliably reported that one of the first persons he baptised was Queen Candace herself.

R.A. Torrey was not only a great preacher but a successful personal soul-winner committed to witnessing at every opportunity. Once when he was walking down a crowded street in Chicago he felt the impulse to speak to a passing man. Pausing briefly while he prayerfully checked the impulse he turned, overtook the stranger and laying his hand upon his shoulder asked: 'My friend, are you a Christian?' The man was startled and Torrey hastened to explain that he did not ask every stranger that question. Conversation soon revealed that the man was in great spiritual need and was already prepared, having been but shortly before challenged on the same issue by a Christian cousin! Torrey's talk proved a further step towards a decision which later followed.

John Wesley was another inveterate personal soul-winner who believed in seeking to win people to Christ at every opportunity. On one occasion when he was riding along on horseback he was joined by another horseman. They soon struck up a conversation and the man (not knowing to whom he was speaking) began to speak against that 'terrible man John Wesley'. After letting the man talk for a little while, Wesley disclosed his identity, whereupon the man tried to gallop off. But people did not get away from Wesley so easily and he pursued him. Wesley said, 'I soon caught up with him for I had the better horse...' and he engaged him in conversation about Christ. Faith sees the opportunity in every difficulty whereas unbelief can only see the difficulty in every opportunity.

The third fishing incident in Peter's life was during the momentous forty days after the resurrection. Once again Peter and his friends had fished all night without catching anything. At dawn a mysterious person on the shore told them, 'Cast the net on the right side of the ship and you will find' (John 21:6). This time the remarkable thing about their catch was that it consisted only of big fish. Immediately the perceptive John recognised the person as Jesus. When they eventually landed the catch Peter was so impressed with the quality and size of the fish that he counted them and found there were one hundred and fifty-three. He also recognised and appreciated another miracle – this time, for all that there were so many fish the net did not break.

In this instance Christ directed operations from the shore, not the boat. He was teaching Peter that He would still be directing their soul-winning activities after His ascension. Though they would not be able to see Him, He would still be able to see them and direct their service. Peter had learned his lessons well. After the Ascension of Christ, Peter stayed in Jerusalem, as commanded, until he was mantled with power from on high. When he let down his net it was filled with a record catch of three thousand new converts who gladly submitted to baptism and continued steadfastly in the faith (Acts 2:41).

When the Spirit is allowed to lead, nothing is impossible, I was called up as an eighteen-year-old in 1944 to do my National Service during the last war. I was in Northern Ireland for a period but in 1946 I had a strong impression that the Lord wanted me in London. I spoke to my Captain but he said it was impossible; very emphatically he told me that even if I got a posting it would certainly not be London. I was a mere corporal, he wanted to keep me and promote me to sergeant; he made it very clear that he did not like soldiers who refused promotion.

But God was in it, and I was transferred to London. I knew that the call of God was on my life and my one ambition was to prepare myself for the ministry. My posting took me to central London where I found a wonderful spiritual home at Peniel Chapel, in Kensington, half a mile or so from Notting Hill. It was then a flourishing independent Pentecostal Church over three hundred strong. The pastor, Benjamin Griffiths, had pioneered the work following his move to London soon after the Welsh Revival. Though he was approaching eighty years of age, he was still a force to be reckoned with. When he first came to London he had a Dairy and in the early days of the work there was such a spirit of revival that it was a common occurrence for customers to 'fall down unto the power of God' and have to be carried into the room behind the shop!

Ben Griffiths had a great burden for souls. He prayed for helpers and when he could not get men, God gave him women to help him in the work. Wonderful women they were too – Miss Evans, Miss Sidford, Miss McIntyre, and Miss Baker. They led the nightly meetings at the world famous Speakers' Corner, Hyde Park, every evening. Talk about 'that was the week that was' – they had an open-air meeting in Hyde Park every night of the week except Friday, followed by a service back at the chapel in Kensington. Though still in the army, my posting to a temporary branch of the War Office (dealing with the resettlement of Polish army doctors) had very easy office hours and after a short period I was allowed to live out of the barracks. I had complete freedom. I knew it was the Lord's doing and it was marvellous in my eyes.

For the eighteen months I was in London I was involved in the open air meetings at Speakers' Corner in Hyde Park, every weekday except Friday, and I usually 'gave a word' under the watchful eye of one or other of these great ladies. It was there in that toughest of schools, notorious for its hecklers, that I felt that I finished my apprenticeship in the art of open-air preaching. We always endeavoured to take those who expressed interest back to the chapel for the service. My contacts included all classes from a high-up official in the Trade Union Movement to a Muslim diplomat in the Iranian Embassy. 'All the world and his wife' came to Speakers' Corner and on Saturdays there were two more meetings, one in the afternoon, and then the greatest one of the week in the evening. Sundays at Peniel started at 6.30 a.m. with a prayer meeting, followed by a street open-air at 9.30 a.m., before the morning service. In the afternoon there was Sunday School and Bible Class, tea at the chapel for all who wanted to stay, then the choice of two open-airs, one in Hyde Park, and another near a cinema in the locality, followed by the evening gospel service. In summer, just for good measure, there was another open-air at 8 p.m. I was at every one and thought it was terrific. I was learning about soul-winning from some of the most dedicated soul-winners I have ever met.

Even now when I think of Ben Griffiths my heart warms. He was a great man of faith. His vision was for the world and his burden to 'by all means – save some.' He believed in the power of the printed word as well as the spoken word and he made Peniel Chapel a centre for the distribution of free tracts. Thousands upon thousand were sent out freely by post to Christian workers who wrote in. No offerings were ever asked for, he relied on God to work through prayer. No offerings were ever taken up in the chapel; there were boxes around the chapel where people could put in their gifts and they did – without ever being prompted from the platform that I can remember. Peniel Chapel also sent out and supported their own missionaries in Brazil, Egypt, Belgium and China. Everything was 'by faith'. Mr Griffiths told me that at one time in the early days of the missionary work there was a financial crisis. As he prayed he felt that God spoke very clearly into his heart: 'You see that the money goes out right and I will see that it comes in all right.' He never worried after that; he knew that, providing he was a good steward, God would take care of everything. Only eternity will reveal just how many people were reached through the faith of Ben Griffiths and his people at Peniel Chapel.

When the time came for me to be discharged from the army at the completion of my National Service I was deeply moved and encouraged when the great old man invited me to his house for a meal – a very rare privilege indeed. He told me that he had some money of his own coming to him for war damage on some property he owned and if I would stay on at Peniel for another year he would send me out evengelising. I prayed about it but did not feel free to accept and God led me in other directions. But in my first two or three years in the ministry we exchanged correspondence regularly and he greatly helped me and inspired me. Every letter was a challenge to greater faith.

When I got married three years later, I spent the first few days of my honeymoon with my new bride in London. We stayed in the Tower of London with 'Beefeater' William Tubby and his wife, who were members at Peniel and great soul-winners. William had been a regular soldier and was a sergeant-major. He was wonderfully converted towards the end of his military career and he and his wife immediately became great personal soul-winners. When William was accepted as a Yeoman of the Guard at the Tower he turned it to good account, using every opportunity to witness wisely but fearlessly for Jesus. As a 'Beefeater' he acted as a guide to the endless stream of visitors to the Tower. To go on a guided tour with him was an experience in itself in how to witness. He knew his history – he made it live and he always managed to put in an effective witness for Christ. He and his wife would also be up early in the morning and at the nearby tube station giving out tracts to the hundreds of workers as they streamed by. At the rehearsal for the funeral service of King George VI in Westminster Abbey, William Tubby was lined up with the rest of the Beefeaters in their ceremonial uniform. When the minister read the words 'I am the Resurrection and the Life' – all the Beefeaters sprang to attention. The officer in charge was angry and wanted to know who had given the order to stand to attention? William Tubby stepped forward and 'owned up' – 'Sir, it was my fault; I always stand to attention when they say that my Lord is the Resurrection and the Life.' It was a bold witness which none of his colleagues could ever foget, especially when shortly afterwards William Tubby died of cancer.

Staying with such a couple it seemed the most natural thing to my precious wife Hazel and myself to spend the first day of our honeymoon, Sunday, in busy service for Jesus at Peniel Chapel. Hazel sang, I preached, and yes – we participated in the open-air at Speakers' Corner in Hyde Park. Ben Griffiths words will be with me to the end of my days. One day he looked at me and said with an authority that brooked no disobedience: 'Young man, make full proof of your ministry.'

Times have altered and methods have changed, but the Holy Spirit is always contemporary in the highest sense. He is always in touch with the present situation in society and if we are in touch with Him – He will lead us to souls who are ready to respond.

Chapter Eight

Faith for the miraculous

Miracles are the footprints of the Almighty. Signs and wonders are the Royal Standard indicating to all that God is in the midst of His people (1 Corinthians 14:25). The supernatural gifts of the Spirit are an indication that God has entered the fight against sin and Satan.

If ever there was a day that cried out for the miraculous in the Christian Church it is this one. The upsurge of the occult, witchcraft, and obsession with Eastern religions, have made the West a front line missionary situation. The only effective answer is the gospel of our Lord Jesus Christ, preached in the power of the Holy Spirit, and confirmed with 'signs following' (Mark 16:15-20). Christ promised, 'These signs shall follow those that believe.' Christ is looking for people of faith who will believe him for the miraculous, and he is finding most of them among 'the poor of this world, rich in faith,' in the Third World, while we in the West continue to be the rich of this world, poor in faith. It is not by chance that Mark, immediately before the Great Commission, tells us how the Risen Christ 'upbraided the eleven for their unbelief and hardness of heart, because they believed not them which had seen him after he had risen' (Mark 16:15).

Unbelief is as infectious as the plague. It can spread through a whole community of God's people in no time at all, as Moses found to his cost when the spies returned from viewing Canaan. Only two out of the ten had any faith – Joshua and Caleb – who declared: These people in

Canaan 'are bread for us, their defence is departed from them, and the Lord is with us: fear them not' (Numbers 14:9).

Fortunately, faith is also 'catching'. I have found throughout my life that faith thrives in the company of people of faith. As a young probationary minister in Assemblies of God in Lancashire I was fortunate to mix with some outstanding people of faith. One such was Fred Watson, the pioneer pastor of the Blackburn Assembly of God. At our District Council meetings whenever he conducted the morning devotions my faith soared – I left ready to tackle anything, I felt ten feet tall. Some of his words have lived with me and inspired me, because, like Stephen he was a man full of faith and the Holy Ghost (Acts 6:5). Commenting on the report of the ten spies he said, 'Joshua and Caleb stood up before the great congregation and encouraged them to go in and possess the land flowing with milk and honey, declaring, "They are bread for us – they may be giants but the Lord is with us and in His name we will make them into sandwiches and eat them up for tea." '

People of faith know how to laugh at impossibilities. Faith revels in an atmosphere of joyous happiness where people are not afraid to laugh. Joy is second only to love in the list of the fruit of the Spirit (Galatians 5:22). Note well any people of faith that you are fortunate enough to meet, cherish their friendship, for you never know when you will need it.

John G. Lake, in the view of many of his contemporaries, exercised one of the greatest ministries of the miraculous of his day, first as a missionary in South Africa and later in Spokane, Washington, USA, where one hundred thousand healings were recorded in five years. Yet, at a crucial moment when he was first entering into a ministry of divine healing, if he had not been able to contact a man full of faith and power, his faith might have been stultified for the rest of his life.

One of his sisters, who was a little older than himself, and to whom he was particularly close, was haemorrhaging badly and dying. His mother contacted him and told he must return home immediately if he wanted to see his favourite sister before she died. He hurried home but was greeted with his mother saying, 'You are too late, she is gone.' He put his hand on her forehead and it was cold, he tried her pulse but could feel nothing, and he put a small mirror to her mouth but there was no sign of breath or life. He was stunned – she was leaving a broken-hearted husband and a little baby. Somehow he felt that he could not let this happen. He walked up and down the room praying, longing for someone with faith in God that he could get to help him. But divine healing was then frowned upon by most of the churches and only a few brave souls had ventured into it.

John Lake could think of only one man who had the kind of faith he needed in his desperate situation. That man was the controversial character, John Alexander Dowie, the founder of Zion City, a Christian community in Illinois, six hundred miles away. John Lake sent Dowie this telegram: 'My sister has apparently died but my spirit will not let her go. I believe that if you will pray, God will heal her.' Dowie wired back. 'Hold on to God. I am praying. She will live.'

John Lake declared: 'I have said a thousand times what it would have meant if instead of that telegram of faith, I had received one from a weakling preacher who might have said: "I am afraid you are on the wrong track," or "Brother, you are becoming fanatical; the days of miracles are past." '

That telegram inspired Lake to pray 'the prayer of faith' (James 5:15). In the name of Jesus Christ he rebuked the sickness and death and pronounced that she would live. As he finished praying he saw his sister's eyelids flutter. Breathlessly he watched for further signs of life and shortly afterwards with his brother-in-law at his side, they saw her eyelids move again. Within five days she was well enough to sit down with the family for their Christmas dinner.

Later John Lake joined Dr. Dowie at Zion City and became an elder. His faith continued to grow and he launched out on some evangelistic and healing crusades which were wonderfully owned of God in the salvation of souls and miracles of healing. Sadly, Dr. Dowie, who had been a tremendous man of faith and one of the early pioneers of the ministry of healing, ended his days with a somewhat tarnished reputation. As an evangelist he was supreme, but when he withdrew from the masses and tried to create a totally separate Christian community he made his big mistake. The crisis came when he strayed from his God-given gifts of healing-evangelism and ventured into various commercial enterprises and banking, the collapse of which brought disrepute upon him and his community. Nevertheless he inspired not only Lake but many others destined to become great evangelists, who learned, from his mistakes as well as from his achievements.

In 1908 Lake felt a very definite call to South Africa to missionary work, and ventured forth in faith, with his wife and their seven children. Within a short time of landing there he was instrumental under God in bringing about a great revival with outstanding miracles and above all, the salvation of many hundreds of souls. At times he and his wife were kept so busy praying for people, not only in the meetings, but in their home, that they had no time to eat.

Lake was no teacher but he was a terrific evangelist, forthright and fearless. He had a friend with him called Tom Hezmelhalch who was an ideal foil to Lake, being a gifted teacher with a gentle spirit of love. In their meetings they would often preach 'in tandem'. If Lake was preaching and Hezmelhalch felt he had not made it clear enough he would step forward and say, 'Wait a bit, John, let me explain that point'. After a few minutes it would be Lake's turn to call out: 'Now hold on a while, Brother Tom, while I clinch that point.' It was a unique partnership. Oftentimes they would each speak five or six times in the course of a meeting but it blended together perfectly because it was all one ministry in the Spirit.

Dr. Dowie opposed the early Pentecostals but Lake had experienced a definite Pentecostal baptism of power and believed in the gifts of the Spirit. Miracles, healings, tongues, interpretation of tongues, prophecy, faith, discerning of spirits, words of wisdom, and words of knowledge, all were manifested on occasions in the revival in Johannesburg.

A Chinese evangelist who had come to South Africa to evangelise his fellow-countrymen in the gold and diamond mines came along to the meetings. He found them so different from the usual evangelical meetings to which he was accustomed that he found himself in a quandary. Lifting his heart to God as he sat in the revival meeting he prayed that God would show him clearly and unmistakably whether this was His work. A moment later a little white girl came and stood in front of him and said, in perfect Chinese, 'This work is of God.' He had spoken to no-one but God and the fact that she was miraculously led straight to him, and had answered the question that was in his heart, in perfect Chinese of which she had no knowledge, convinced him of the genuineness of the revival. He sought and received the baptism of the Holy Spirit and returned to China to evangelise.

Lake's forthright preaching often aroused violent opposition and his life was threatened on occasions but God protected him. One night an enraged mob entered the hall with pick handles and other weapons, saying they were going to 'do' the preacher. Lake and his friend continued to preach and pray as usual and at the end of the service Lake walked quietly and lovingly up to the mob. Holding out his hand to them he said, 'God bless you,' and proceeded to walk unscathed through the midst of them.

A detective from the Johannesburg CID went along to the meetings to investigate and was amazed to see many of the city's noted criminals not only in the meetings but flocking out to the front for salvation. Many of them were gloriously saved and lived changed lives.

One great miracle which impressed the city was the healing of a chronic cripple called Charlie. During the course of his life he had suffered a series of accidents, starting in boyhood when he was hit on the head with a stone from a catapult. Later his hand was caught in a machine, severing the tendons of the wrist. Then his foot and leg were crushed by a heavy pulley which fell on him. He was married with a baby girl but life was hard, especially for his wife. After months in Johannesburg hospital he was discharged as incurable. He felt so useless that he contemplated suicide.

Then he heard about Lake's meetings and he went along there on his crutches. The power of God went through him when Lake prayed for him and he was healed instantly. He threw away his crutches and the crowd cheered as Charlie ran and jumped for joy. He ran home to tell his wife who had gone to bed. She was awakened by the noise of someone jumping around in the dining-room. She was afraid thinking that a crazy drunkard had broken into the house. Fearfully she crept downstairs. Peering round the door she was amazed to see her husband, Charlie, vaulting backwards and forwards across the table and shouting for joy.

Miracles such as this brought the crowds and thousands were saved and healed but, for all that, Lake and his family were on the poverty line; people thought that he must have plenty of support from America, whereas in fact they were literally penniless. Such was their dedication that they refused to make their needs known, but it took its toll, especially of Mrs Lake, and she died some months later.

Another outstanding miracle concerned a gold-miner called Swanepoel whose eye had burst when a blasting cartridge accidently exploded in his face. They rushed him to the hospital where the doctors wanted to remove the remains of the damaged eye. Swanepoel asked if he could be taken to Lake for prayer first. He was in agony as Lake and a group of Christians took him into the prayer room. The dressing was removed and as Lake prayed for him, to the wonderment of those present they saw the scattered fragments of the eye drawn together as by an unseen hand. By the time Lake said 'Amen' the pain was gone and the eye was perfectly whole.

Lake fearlessly fought racial prejudice which was already strong way back in 1908 in South Africa. A coloured preacher called Letwaba, who had been trained and accepted by the Lutherans, was hungry for God and reality. He was disillusioned by the missionaries of his acquaintance, many of whom drank and smoked; sin was tolerated and even adultery condoned. After three years with the Berlin Mission and nineteen with the Bapedi Lutherans he was desperate to find the truth. He was directed to Lake's meetings and immediately sensed that at last he was to find it. When he went out for prayer Lake put his arm around him, kissed him and called him 'brother', which roused the wrath of many of the unconverted whites in the meeting and they booed Lake. Lake rounded on them and declared with authority, 'God has made of one blood all nations of men' (Acts 17:26). 'If you don't acknowledge them as your brothers you will go into eternal woe and will see these black folk going to eternal bliss.' At this the shouting and hissing increased and some were so incensed they shouted: 'Put out the black devils. Kick them into the street.' Lake stood firmly by Letwaba and with his arm still around his shoulder he told them, 'If you put this man and his friends out then you must turn me out too, for I will stand by my black brethren.'

Letwaba was accustomed to being insulted especially by the Boers. It was new to him to hear a white preacher declaring his love for him. He knew his quest for the truth was over. Very soon he was baptised with the Holy Spirit, speaking in other tongues. He became a mighty evangelist to his own people. He learned much from Lake and eventually he started the Patmos Bible School and was mightily used among the black folk in Northern Transvaal. 'Signs and wonders' followed his preaching and at least twice it was claimed that the dead were raised. William F.P. Burton, the famous pioneer missionary and founder of the Congo Evangelistic Mission, became his friend and was so impressed by him that he wrote the story of Letwabas life under the title *When God Makes a Pastor*. Mr Burton's name gained world-wide respect as a man of the highest integrity and he declared that he had 'taken considerable pains to verify incidents and to assure accuracy in detail'. People of faith such as Lake start a kind of faith chain-reaction, which goes on from generation to generation, as in the case of Letwaba.

Whenever divine healing is mentioned then invariably the question is asked: 'What about those not healed?' Jesus, with a wisdom that was 'from above' as opposed to that which is 'earthly and natural' (James 3:15), often answered his critics' question with another question. When the chief priests asked: 'By what authority doest thou these things?' Jesus countered: 'I will also ask of you one question, and answer me, and I will tell you by what authority I do these things. The baptism of John, was it from heaven, or of men?' They could not, would not, dare answer Him and so He silenced them (Mark 11:27-33).

The question is not: 'What about the unhealed?' but 'what about divine healing – is it scriptural?'

When a young clergyman tried to involve the Duke of Wellington into solving an argument he got more than he bargained for. He asked the Iron Duke, 'Is it possible to preach the gospel to every person in the world?' and got the unexpected answer: 'Look to your marching orders in the gospels – what do they say? "Preach the gospel to every creature" – so stop arguing and get on with it or you may be in trouble with your great commander.'

Is healing a part of the commission of Christ? Most reasonable people feel that the latter part of Mark's gospel has been more than verified and for all such there can be no further argument. These are their marching orders: 'Go you into all the world and preach the gospel to every creature... and these signs shall follow them that believe... they shall lay hands on the sick and they shall recover' (Mark 16:15-17). I do not think that the Lord will hold us responsible for those not healed; I do feel very strongly, however, that He will hold us responsible if we do not carry out His orders, including laying hands on the sick in His name.

Have the gifts of the Spirit been withdrawn from the Church? Some vainly try to cover their prejudice against tongues by twisting and quoting out of context 'tongues... shall cease' (1 Corinthians 13:8). Of course the gift of tongues will cease but not until 'that which is perfect is come', not until 'we know even as we are known' (1 Corinthians 13:8,12). Has modern medicine made healing obsolete? One might as well ask whether education for all in Britain has made the preaching of the gospel unnecessary. 'The gifts of healings' are as permanent a part of the church as apostles, prophets and teachers, all of which are 'set' in the church by God Himself (1 Corinthians 12:28). We have too 'the prayer of faith' by the elders of the local church in James 5:14-16. As long as it is right to pray for the souls of men (v. 19,20); as long as it is right for the afflicted to resort to prayer (v. 13); for so long will be it right to anoint the sick with the oil in the name of the Lord and pray over them – and that will be until the Lord returns and 'this mortal puts on immortality' (1 Corinthians 15:54).

Healing has rightly been called the handmaid of the gospel for in many cases it opens doors and hearts which otherwise would remain closed to the message of saving grace.

What about those puzzling cases where healing does not take place? I have a bigger question – for the salvation of the soul is of greater importance than the healing of the body. What about those who respond to the gospel message and then 'go back' or make a decision but show no fruits of the new birth in their life? What about the believer who falls into sin? Has the gospel failed? We know the answer to that – the gospel cannot fail. 'It is the power of God unto salvation to every one that believeth' – but every evangelist and pastor has experienced disappointing cases for which there is no human explanation. Nevertheless, we do not stop preaching the gospel, but rather we re-examine our preaching and our methods, our counselling and our praying so that, humanly speaking, we do out utmost to ensure that the cause of failure cannot be laid at our door.

I have served as a pastor for over thirty years and I am thoroughly acquainted with the problems associated with follow-up after crusades, both the straightforward evangelistic variety and the evangelism and healing species. Looking back I have no regrets at any crusade relating to any of the churches I have pastored, but I am now sorry that I did not have more crusades on a regular basis as part of a whole programme of continuous evangelism in the local church. Indeed, in my present church, I have just persuaded the church council to build in a major evangelistic and healing crusade every year for the next three years. In spite of disappointments I still believe in evangelism and evangelists. I can see abiding fruit and lasting healings from many such efforts and therefore I prefer to ask: 'What about the healed? What about the saved? Would you deny them their healing? Would you deny them their salvation?'

A medical doctor who believes in divine healing said, 'I have the complete conviction that there is no such thing as an incurable disease; that there is no such thing as a false hope of healing in His Name and that no one need die in pain. I have that conviction, and I express it, and I act on it. In true healing there is no name that has anything like the power of the name of Jesus Christ; the mention of that name in healing produces miracles and daily I have been privileged to see new revelations of what it means (Dr Christopher Woodard, an Anglican, in *A Doctor Heals By Faith*, Parrish 1953).

I believe in doctors and medicines and believe it is right for them to pursue their quest for cures for the various ills which plague mankind. A panel of over two hundred medical scientists said at the beginning of 1987 they believe a cure will be found for two out of three people with cancer by the year 2000 but an effective remedy for the common cold is unlikely. It is interesting that they say they expect the cure rate for cancer to increase as a result of steady research rather than by any sudden dramatic breakthrough. They also say that prevention is the most important way of curbing cancer, notably by reducing smoking and watching diet. The majority of cancers are now regarded as preventable. (Quoted in *The Independent*, 10 March 1987).

Another doctor who had come to accept divine healing said, 'It is now very clear to me that our profession generally takes a completely materialistic view towards diseases and this fact alone makes it impossible to cure many diseases.' John Wesley wrote: 'Why do doctors go on treating patients with physic when they need the care of a minister?' The medical profession ignores divine healing at its peril; and the church and those who believe in divine healing reject the medical profession to their detriment. Both sides have much to learn from each other.

I believe that the increase in the effectiveness of divine healing will likewise come about by the steady restoration of spiritual power in the church through disciplined prayer, study of the scriptures, the consistent building of relationships, and commitment to world evangelism, rather than by any sudden visitation of God – though revival and revivals will play their part. In Paul Yonggi Cho's great church in Seoul, for example, it is now claimed that seventy per cent of all sick people who go to Prayer Mountain are healed. No healings are claimed until they have been checked out by medical doctors.

The case still on every thinking Christian's lips is that of the greatly loved and deeply mourned David Watson. With the prayers of so many thousands for this choice servant of God not bringing about his deliverance from the cancer of which he died, what can we say that has not already been said a thousand times? I was privileged to have close fellowship with David over several years at the Charismatic Leaders' Conference and the more I got to know him the more I esteemed him and appreciated his gentleness, humility and faith. His last book *Fear No Evil*, written under the shadow of imminent death from cancer, may yet prove to be the greatest contribution of his fruitful life.If anyone could have been excused for losing faith in divine healing it would have been David's wife, Anne.

Instead we find her, with great courage, back at York at their old church, serving as an elder. Her special responsibility is for the ministry of spiritual gifts and so she is teaching and training people to pray for the sick. She says: 'I had always avoided the healing ministry. When David was dying, I felt as if I had a bow and arrow, what I really needed was an Exocet missile. After his death, I said, "Lord, whatever it takes, I'll learn to pray for the sick." So I got into the kindergarten. Now I'm getting everyone else there. It'a a powerful area, especially in evangelism.'

Chapter Nine

The Language of Faith

When I was asked to write the Foreword to *Plundering Hell*, the story of Reinhard Bonnke, I wrote: 'In the last five years the faith of two men has staggered me. In my presence I have heard them say what they felt God wanted them to achieve – and I ranked it as impossible. Those two men were Yonggi Cho and Reinhard Bonnke. Now I have lived to see the fulfilment of both of their faith dreams.

'In the case of Yonggi Cho he said he was believing God for a church of half a million people. (It was then less than half that – a mere two hundred thousand or so!) He has now passed that target. In the case of Reinhard Bonnke he was talking about creating the world's biggest tent, capable of seating over 34,000 people. The technical difficulties alone were enough to deter any ordinary individual, let alone the financial costs. But the book was published to coincide with the opening and dedication of the worlds biggest mobile tent in 1984 and my unbelief was suitably rebuked.'

Soon after its erection it was blown down and destroyed, but Bonnke with typical courage and faith soon had it replaced and filled over and over again as he set about his task of taking the gospel in that tent from the Cape to Cairo. Three years later, as he continues to move up through that great African continent, there is only one problem: the world's biggest tent is already too small for the crowds he is attracting. Reinhard Bonnke is now using stadiums where they are available, or even open fields. However, he reckons the tent is just about the right size for Europe and he is planning to use it for great meetings across Europe in between his African crusades.

Bonnke and Cho are living proofs that 'what you can conceive you can achieve.' Real faith is never satisfied with its achievements, it is always expanding its horizons and pressing forward for more. People of faith utter a fervent 'Amen' to the prayer of the apostles when they said to Jesus: 'Lord, increase our faith' (Luke 17:10). Listen to people of faith and you will find they are always talking faith and they are always positive. They watch every word they say because they know that the battle is so often won or lost by that little member – the tongue. James rightly warns us that 'the tongue is a fire, a world of iniquity... it is set on fire of hell. It is an unruly evil, full of deadly poison' (3:6,8). Satan knows this and does everything he can to get unbelief to major on negative confession. It is destructive and harmful.

The Holy Spirit knows the creative power of the tongue and on the Day of Pentecost the yielded tongues of the one hundred and twenty were set on fire of heaven. Peter's inspired words were the antidote to the deadly poison of sin, creating faith and ministering healing.

I will never forget hearing Reinhard Bonnke tell how God pushed him into the ministry of the miraculous. After several years of plodding away at routine missionary work, he arranged for an outstanding evangelist with a healing ministry to conduct a weekend crusade in Lesotho. Bonnke spent a lot of money advertising the meetings and prayed much for a break through in that difficult and hard area. The church was packed out but the evangelist departed after only one meeting, leaving Bonnke in the lurch. Bonnke was upset and as he drove to the meeting he cried to God and said, 'I am just a missionary, one of your little men.' As he started preaching he felt that God was speaking to him and saying: 'My words in your mouth are just as powerful as any words in my own mouth.' He was staggered at the revelation but as he considered it he realised that the power was in the Word of God. It was the beginning of his ministry of signs and wonders when the blind were healed and a cripple child was made whole.

I must confess that as I listened to him telling that story, once again I found myself 'staggered by my unbelief'. But as I prayerfully considered the matter I began to see that it was scriptural. For example, Jesus said to the seventy as he sent them out to preach: 'He that heareth you heareth me' (Mark 10:16).

At creation, formlessness, emptiness, and darkness prevailed; and even though the Spirit of God brooded over it, until God *spoke* – nothing happened. As soon as he said, 'Let there be light: there was light' (Genesis 1:3). 'Through faith we understand that the worlds were framed by the word of God' (Hebrews 11:3). The word of God has creative power.

The written word and the spoken word are an integral part of faith. Our speech directly impacts our faith. Educationalists tell us that we remember only ten per cent of what we hear, but ninety per cent of what we actually say. The steps to faith then are; first, prayerfully read the Word: second, believe the Word and receive it in our hearts: third, speak it out and act upon it.

It goes without saying, of course, that one must always 'rightly divide the word of truth' (2 Timothy 2:15), which means not taking it out of context. We must never 'wrest the scriptures' (2 Peter 3:16). The picture there is of torturing the scriptures, putting them on the rack as it were and stretching them unmercifully, as they did in mediaeval times when they put their victims on the rack. Unfortunately this is what is happening in some extreme forms of so-called positive confession teaching, with tragic results in some cases. For those not familiar with this teaching it relies on a dictionary definition of 'confess': 'to own or admit; to acknowledge fully, to acknowledge faith in.' It goes further than what has always been acknowledged as the legitimate perimeters of scriptural teaching on confession. It divides into negative and positive areas. The negative is acknowledging sin, poverty, sickness, or anything unpleasant. The positive admits or owns only the pleasant things. The inference is definitely given that by concentrating on the positive you can enjoy anything and everything that is pleasant, including health, riches, and possessions. All you have to do to avoid the unpleasant things of life is to refrain from making any negative confessions.

As always the answer lies, not in rejecting out of hand all forms of positive confession teaching, but in coming to a balanced scriptural viewpoint, by considering all the scriptures on the subject and comparing scripture with scripture. Confession is an important and powerful truth, Satan knows that, and it is why he seeks to drive people into extreme positions where they bring the doctrine into disrepute.

We must pray that God will give us the spirit of faith like Paul who wrote: 'We have the same spirit of faith, according as it is written, I believed and therefore I have spoken; we also believe and therefore speak' (2 Corinthians 4:13). Paul here is quoting from Psalm 116:10 where the psalmist was in dire straits: 'The sorrows of death compassed him, the pains of hell got hold upon him and he found trouble and sorrow' (v. 3). He was brought low (v. 6) but God helped him and in spite of all, he still believed and never lost his grip on God throughout his trouble (v. 10). Spurgeon and others are agreed that it was the Spirit of Christ prophetically at work in the psalmist, and Christ himself is actually foreseen in the psalm as oppressed and stricken but still trusting and believing even for resurrection,. Faith must always speak out, and it has to speak *before* it happens, not *afterwards*.

Paul had come to this same spirit of faith. Although he was really going through it at that particular time he could say, 'we are troubled but not distressed; perplexed but not in despair; persecuted but not forsaken; cast down but not destroyed' (2 Corinthians 4:8,9). Faith is often knocked down – but never knocked out. Faith always gets up before the devil can count it 'out'. Faith 'faints not' (v. 1), in other words, it never gives up.

Faith is not afraid of setting a 'faith-goal' and declaring it before anything happens. Almost twenty-five years ago, when I was a young pastor in Radcliffe, on the outskirts of Manchester, I first learned about setting a faith-goal. The one who taught me this was a man with a tremendous passion for souls and a white-hot burning zeal for God. His name was John Nelson Parr, and he played the key role in founding the Fellowship of Assemblies of God in Great Britain and Ireland. An evangelistic pastor, he succeeded in building up what was for many years the largest Pentecostal Church in Britain at Levenshulme, Manchester, with a membership around the thousand mark. Inspired by his example, I felt we should set ourselves a target as a church in our silver jubilee year of winning at least twenty-five souls for Christ. Our congregation was then around fifty to fifty-five and so it was quite a target, but with God's help we achieved it. In around six years we saw the church congregation on a Sunday evening treble to around the one hundred and seventy mark. If I had kept the goal a secret, afraid to declare it, I am sure that we would not have gained our twenty-five souls, and if we had not gained that objective we would not have set ourselves other growth-goals. I only regret that after leaving Radcliffe somehow I let that lesson slip away from me. Now I am back to setting faith-goals again.

A lot has been said recently about the *rhema* word and the *logos* word. Those teaching it strongly claim there is a difference between these two Greek words. It is claimed that *logos* refers to the written word and *rhema* to that which is presently spoken by faith. According to this view, whatever is spoken by faith becomes inspired and takes on the creative power of God. Many Bible scholars, however,

however, maintain that the distinction is not justified and say the words are used interchangeably. Certainly it is risky to build a whole doctrine upon these two words. However, it is interesting and helpful to find that Dr Ironside in his Greek Lexicon, which was written before the present controversy arose, defines *logos* as 'the said word of God' and *rhema* as 'the saying word of God'. In other words, the *rhema* is when God quickens one or more of his promises to us in a specific situation. This is safe ground and something which preachers have long experienced as they seek the face of God for the message he would have them preach: they know the thrill of God's Spirit bringing a specific scripture to their attention.

Faith never tries to 'twist God's arm' but always seeks the will of God, assured that it is 'good, acceptable, and perfect' (Romans 12:2). It does not accept the extreme positive teaching that 'to admit weakness is to accept defeat; to admit financial need is to accept poverty; and to admit sickness is to preclude healing.' Rather, faith accepts that often 'Christ's strength is made perfect in our weakness' and chooses therefore to 'glory in infirmities that the power of Christ may rest upon us' (2 Corinthians 12:9). Faith seeks always 'to abide in Christ and to let his words abide in us' – knowing that when that is the case, it is safe from selfish desires and Satan's deceptions (John 15:7). Faith then asks with confidence because it knows it desires only what is in line with the will of God.

The language of faith is that of praise, thanksgiving, and worship, not of grumbling, moaning, and groaning. Einstein unlocked the secrets of atomic power with the simple formula $E = MC^2$. Here is a little formula which is the secret of atomic power in prayer: $PP = FPr^2$ – which being interpreted is: Prayer Power equals Faith times Praise squared (or doubled). Prayer without faith is just so much 'empty talk'. 'The missing element that is necessary to energise triumphant faith is *praise* – perpetual, purposeful, aggressive praise,' says Paul Billheimer.

Einstein's formula made atomic power available to the world. Nuclear power brought World War II to a quick close. Nuclear power has taken man into space. Nuclear power is driving our factories and lighting our cities. The key lay in one little formula.

Learn this formula well if you want to increase your prayer power. PP (Prayer Power) = F (Faith) multiplied by Pr^2 (Praise doubled). Not just praise, but praise doubled, praise upon praise. This was one of Paul's open secrets. 'In everything give thanks for this is the will of God in Christ Jesus concerning you' (1 Thessalonians 5:18). Again: 'Giving thanks always for all things unto God and the Father in the name of the Lord Jesus Christ' (Ephesians 5:20). 'Praise the Lord' and 'Hallelujah' may be expressions which are despised on earth but they are highly prized in heaven.

What about speaking in tongues? One cannot talk about the language of faith without referring to this precious gift. Christ himself promised that this would be one of the signs which would follow those who believe: 'They shall speak with new tongues' (Mark 16:17). Of all the gifts of the Spirit this is probably the one which is still least understood and most underestimated. Some still tend to dismiss it as of little account, saying (though on what grounds I am not sure) that 'tongues is the least of the gifts'.

All I can say is that most of the great people of faith that it has been my privilege to know have expressed their ever increasing appreciation of this precious gift. Yonggi Cho says, 'As a young Christian, I could not see the importance of tongues in my Christian life. However, the longer I believe in Jesus Christ, the more I feel the tremendous importance of tongues in my own personal Christian life. I spend a good deal of my prayer life praying in my spiritual language' (*Prayer: Key to Revival,* Word UK Ltd). John Wimber discloses: 'For me, praying in tongues is like putting up my spiritual antennae: my spiritual receptivity increases. 1 Corinthians 14:4 says, "He who speaks in a tongue edifies himself..." That describes my experience. As I speak in tongues I edify myself; I build up my faith and my spiritual sensitivity.' He also mentions that 'everyone I have met who is effective in healing prayer speaks in tongues' (*Power Healing,* Hodder & Stoughton). Not to mention David Wilkerson (of *Cross and the Switchblade* fame) and more recently Jackie Pullinger (*Chasing the Dragon*) and the part that the gift of tongues has played in their rescue work among addicts in New York and Hong Kong respectively.

Clearly, there is much more to tongues speaking than meets the ear! It is possible to pray in tongues and to intercede at a deeper level than would otherwise be possible. It is also a wonderful way of expressing thanks to God, for he understands even when others do not, as Paul says: 'When thou shalt bless with the spirit... thou givest thanks well... ' (1 Corinthians 14:16,17). Although that aspect of it has to be 'controlled' in a meeting, there is no such limitation when one is engaged in private prayer.

Lewi Pethrus, the Swedish Pentecostal patriarch, attained worldwide acceptance as a leader of apostolic stature and wisdom. Wheaton College honoured him with a Doctorate of Divinity in recognition of 'his oustanding spiritual leadership in the cause of Christ throughout the world.' He was made the pastor of a small group of around thirty people in Stockholm in 1910. When he retired some sixty years later, it had nearly seven thousand members and was the largest European Pentecostal Church, supporting over five hundred missionaries around the world. He started a Christian Daily Paper which still flourishes and exercises a considerable national influence, and he had a large part in the worldwide Swedish missionary radio work, IBRA. He majored on soul-winning but he did not neglect the social needs of his times. In the depression years of the 1930's he fed and clothed the poor and needy, and used two remodelled ships for sleeping quarters for the homeless.

His friends marked his seventieth birthday by initiating a special fund called 'The Lewi Pethrus Foundation for Philanthropic Ministry.' This work specialises in helping the drug addicts and alcoholics. All the department heads of the organisation are former addicts or alcoholics who have found salvation and deliverance through Christ. The work has gained national acceptance in Sweden. The testimony of such a man demands respect. I believe his experience of the baptism of the Holy Spirit is especially helpful.

It was while returning to Sweden by boat after a short visit to Norway in 1902 that God first met him. Alone on deck at dawn, after a night of prayer with friends before boarding the vessel, he says: 'Tears streamed down my cheeks. A current of power and sweetness went through my entire being, and I spoke strange words which surprised me a great deal. It was not until the Pentecostal revival broke through and Pastor T.B. Barratt came to Norway with the message about the baptism in the Spirit that I understood what I had experienced on board the ship was the baptism in the Holy Spirit accompanied by this sign of tongues. Because I did not know any teaching concerning the baptism in the Holy Spirit, I never spoke about it. Though I saw great results in conversions through my ministry, no-one received the baptism in the Holy Spirit during the first five years after my experience. I just did not realise that I had experienced the baptism in the Holy Spirit; consequently I could not preach this truth nor teach it.

'This experience of mine has also taught me something that I have often wondered about. We have read about God's messengers throughout the centuries who have been mighty instruments in the hands of the Lord... yet we have never heard that they were baptised in the Holy Spirit. I believe, however, that these did have the baptism in the Holy Spirit. They had the experience although they never realised what it really was. When I had had this experience

I never spoke about it; it seemed so wonderful and sacred that I wanted to keep it for myself. If the Pentecostal revival had not come my way, I would, doubtless, have passed from the earthly scene with this experience hidden in my own heart.

'My concept of the Pentecostal revival, as I was introduced to it in 1907, was an absolutely outstanding event in my life. However, my concept of the experience of the baptism in the Holy Spirit was of such dimensions that the experience I had had on board ship in 1902 all but vanished. I was given the impression that the baptism in the Holy Spirit was something far greater than what I had experienced in my solitude. It was reported that people were smitten to the floor, that they went into ecstasy, and that when speaking in tongues, they lost all conscious control. You see, I had never seen a person receive the baptism in the Holy Spirit, neither had I studied this matter closely in the Bible.

'Later when I saw the manifestations of the Spirit in others I realised that what I experienced in 1902 of the power of God accompanied by speaking in tongues was the baptism in the Holy Spirit. It is not any more remarkable than that. Many people are hindered from receiving the baptism in the Holy Spirit because they are expecting something which, as far as they are concerned, will never come. They are expecting violent outward maifestations, but they are waiting in vain.'

My own experience of the baptism in the Holy Spirit was very similar in some aspects. As a teenager of seventeen I had been earnestly seeking for several months to be filled with the Holy Spirit. I went in every 'tarrying meeting' that was being held but came out feeling further away from receiving than ever. I searched my heart and put everything right that I could, including making restitution of a few exercise books which I had got involved in 'wrongfully acquiring' with some of my friends when still at school in the sixth form. Then one night, praying alone in my bedroom at home, very gently and quietly the Holy Spirit came upon me. After a short while I found myself speaking very quietly 'unknown words'. It was all so simple and relaxed that I could not decide whether 'this was the baptism or not', and so I said nothing about it to anyone.

A couple of days later I started working as a trainee with a senior evangelist called Henry Shave, in the first Home Missions caravan of Assmblies of God. Almost the first question he asked me was 'Have you been baptised in the Holy Spirit?' I mumbled an uncertain 'no'; whereupon almost before I had unpacked my things, he marched me up to the local mission hall, got me down on my knees and started to pray for me. Within minutes I was carrying on exactly where I had left off in my bedroom a couple of nights previous. As I spoke in tongues (still very quietly though clearly) Henry excitedly shouted, 'Hallelujah, you have received...' Like Lewi Pethrus, I was disappointed because I had not received an anticipated remarkable experience with great outward manifestations. However, I soon learned that 'our heavenly Father knows how to give the Holy Spirit to them that ask him' (Luke 11:13). He treats us all individually; he deals with us as sons not clones. Because of the way I had received I more readily came to appreciate that the baptism was the beginning not the end of the Spirit-filled life, and that the emphasis was on receiving the person of the Holy Spirit rather than on the experience itself, or even on the tongues. But I soon came to value tongues as a means 'of perpetuating the baptism' and that appreciation is still increasing over forty years later, in prayer, in praise, and in worship, as well as with the gift of interpretation.

There are times when the gift of tongues seems to be used as a vehicle for other gifts of the Spirit, such as 'revelation or knowledge' as Paul hints at in 1 Corinthians 14:6, and for a supernatural sign. One instance will have to suffice but hundreds could be cited. Radcliffe, near

Manchester, was the scene of my second pastorate. It is on the fringe of 'Coronation Street' country and the people are typically blunt and down-to-earth. Mabel Yates was in her late teens when we had a lovely move of the Holy Spirit in the town following a successful crusade by a Welsh evangelist, Howell Harris. Several engineers at a local power station came to Christ, with their families. Among the colleagues they brought along to our services was a young man called Harry Baron. In a Youth Rendezvous in a home one Sunday evening, Harry made no bones about the fact that he was not a Christian and began to air his philosophy, saying, 'Perhaps we don't really exist at all. Perhaps we only exist as a thought in the mind of some other Being.' Red-headed Lancashire lass Mabel soon demolished his wonderful theory by clouting him quite hard with her hand and saying, 'Aye, you daft thing, you won't feel that then will you if you aren't really here?' Eveybody roared with laughter, but the shaft went home to Harry's heart and it was not long before he surrendered to Christ and became a real help in the Church, doing a great work with a tape recorder, visiting the sick and unsaved with his recordings, at a time when such things were only in their infancy. I have related that incident only to show the kind of person Mabel is.

Some years after I had moved to another pastorate, a former missionary from Zaire called Horace Butler became the minister. At a Saturday evening in 1962 the congregation gave themselves to prayer as the Lord moved upon the meeting. Many of them got down on their knees to show they really meant business with God. Horace Butler had been an outstanding missionary for many years before being forced to leave Zaire following the bloody civil war immediately after Independence, but was always longing to return. I will let him describe what happened next.

'Suddenly, Mabel began to speak in tongues – I was immediately aware that it was Kingwana of the Swahili group used in the southern part of the Zaire Evangelistic Mission Field. She described rushing water and the need of thirsty people and so on. It was clear that she was actually seeing this and I ran and knelt nearby but I could see nothing. I was pondering the use of the lingua-franca and not the pure Kiluba! I knew that God was especially speaking to me, it obviously meant nothing to the rest of the congregation and I knew Mabel had no knowledge of that dialect whatsoever.

'In less than a month we received a cable asking us to return to help the church in the southern area (Luena) of the ZEM work; the very area which uses this language. The scene Mabel described was of the need of these people who were thirsty for the water of life; we knew that we were to be the means of giving it to them.'

Horace Butler and his wife Elsie later served in the chaplaincy in the great Nairobi University for several years. He officially 'retired' in 1985 but in 1987 answered another call to return to Zaire to undertake work with the Bible Society in preparing a translation of the Old Testament. He is a great missionary and a reliable witness. He confirmed the details of this story for me in the writing of this chapter, as did Mabel herself. She says that she remembers that Horace told her it was as though she was 'beseeching' someone; and she recalls that she moved her hands up and down, as though to describe the torrents of water coming down which she 'saw' in a kind of vision. Mabel is now married and her husband is the secretary of the Radcliffe Assembly of God.

Nor is that the end of the story; some months later, another missionary of many years standing, Donald Crook, visited Radcliffe. Donald worked for many years in India, and then in South Africa among the Indians there. In his meeting in Radcliffe, Mabel again spoke in tongues but this time it was in Tamil which was recognised by Donald, and as with Horace, it had special significance for him concerning confirmation of God's leading in his life.

When it comes to being rich in faith we must watch our language. Faith removes such words as 'impossible' from its vocabulary. It is an accepted fact that the few habitual words a person uses most reveal their essential thought pattern. A special friend of mine was privileged to spend a time of close fellowship with Lewi Pethrus. He especially wanted to know how much time Pethrus spent in prayer, expecting to be told by the great man that he spent so many hours every day on his knees. Instead, Pethrus looked at him in surprise and replied: 'How much time do I spend in prayer? I am always praying, yes, I am always praying.' That is the language of faith – unceasing prayer and praise, both with the understanding and with the spirit. One's life is enriched immeasurably as this becomes the daily norm.

Chapter Ten

Faith in the Furnace of Suffering

It may well be that the time is at hand when the Church in the West is going to have to pay its 'back-taxes'. Taxes, that is, in suffering not cash. Peter warned the early church: 'Keep cool, keep awake. Your enemy the devil prowls like a roaring lion, looking out for someone to devour. Resist him; keep your foothold in the faith, *and learn to pay the same tax of suffering as the rest of your brotherhood throughout the world*. Once you have suffered for a little, the God of all grace, who has called you to his eternal glory in Christ Jesus, will repair, recruit, and strengthen you' (1 Peter 5:8-10 Moffatt).

It has been said that salvation is free but you have to pay for everything afterwards, and in some senses that is true. Christ said to the lukewarm church at Laodicea: 'I counsel you to buy of me gold tried in the fire that you may be rich' (Revelation 3:18). He had what they needed but they were going to have to pay for it; he was not going to give it to them. Solomon wisely advised his son: 'Buy the truth and sell it not; also wisdom, and instruction, and understanding' (Proverbs 23:23).

Study is the price that must be paid for knowledge and study has been defined as 'the application of the seat of the trousers to the seat of the chair until the subject has been mastered.' Practice is the price one has to pay for efficiency and accomplishment as every budding musician very soon discovers. Training and exercise is the price one has to pay for athletic achievement. Even the so-called born athletes are not exempt from the cost of regular training as Daley Thompson, Steve Cram, and Seb Coe will all painfully but triumphantly confirm. Olympic gold medals are obtained at the cost of sweat, toil and tears. 'Trials of many kinds' is the price one has to pay for 'faith that is sterling' (Peter 1:6,7 Moffatt). Christ has no bargain basement, no cut-price offers. He loves us too much to try to make things easier for us. That is why He spoke as He did to the mediocre church at Laodicea. He said, 'As many as I love, I rebuke and chasten: be zealous therefore and repent' (3:19).

Laodicea was a successful commercial and financial centre, a city of wealthy bankers and fabulous shopping centres. Gold from the interior was refined at Laodicea and the bankers boasted of the city's riches and their ability to meet all demands made upon them. Jesus, therefore, was speaking to the church in their own language when he talked about 'gold tried in the fire'. They were experts in gold and there were many lessons to be learned from it.

Gold is almost indestructible. It is impervious to the ravages of time, is not tarnished by air or water, and is unaffected by most corrosives. 'The acid test' refers to the practice of jewellers putting a drop of acid on any metal purporting to be gold. Gold bears the imprint of eternity and so does real faith. Gold is more ductile and malleable than any other metal. It has been hammered into sheets as thin as 250,000th of an inch. A little gold goes a long way – and so does a small amount of real faith: a grain of mustard seed of it is enough to move a mountain.

Revelation opens with the picture of the churches as a seven-stemmed golden lampstand with the Risen and Glorified Christ walking in the midst. The lampstand first appeared in the Tabernacle of Moses and was located in the holy place. It was made out of one talent of pure gold, which was 114 pounds in weight. It was a type of Christ as the Light both of His people and of the world and was a lampstand, fed with oil. When God gave Moses directions as to its making, he was told that it was not to be cast but to be made of 'beaten work' (Exodus 25:31). This was possible because of the malleable properties of gold, and the anointed skill of Bezaleel produced this beautiful piece of workmanship with the bowls made like almonds with a bud and a flower in each stem. Beaten work speaks of suffering. In Revelation the teaching has progressed to the point where Christ and His church have become so united as to be similarly identified and virtually inseparable. The message is clear: the servant is not above his master; the church is not above her head. It is significant that the oil for the lampstand was to be 'pure oil olive beaten for the light, to cause the lamp to burn always' (Exodus 27:20). There is no escaping the message: suffering is inevitable if the church would share the glory of her Lord. 'The captain of our salvation was made perfect through sufferings (Hebrews 2:10).

Gethsemane means 'olive press'; and it was not only that dark night before Calvary that Christ went to the garden, for we read 'he oft-times resorted thither with his disciples' (John 18:2). His whole life was one of suffering: 'he was a man of sorrows and acquainted with grief' (Isaiah 53:3). There is no way that the Church can experience 'the power of his resurrection' without sharing also 'in the fellowship of his suffering' (Philippians 3:10).

It is a fact of life that those who suffer most are those who make the biggest impact on society. It is a fact of spiritual life that 'all that will live godly in Christ Jesus shall suffer persecution' (2 Timothy 3:12). 'Gold tried in the fire' is literally 'fired (and fresh) from the fire,' i.e. just fresh from the furnace which has proved its purity. The greater the heat, the better its quality.

When buying gold jewellery, a pressed-in quality mark tells the purchaser how much gold they are actually getting. The portion of pure gold is expressed in carats, with twenty-four representing pure gold. An eighteen carat gold ring is made of eighteen parts of gold and six of alloy. A nine carat ring has only nine parts of gold and fifteen parts of alloy. That's why my wife insisted on a twenty-two carat ring for her wedding day, while a nine carat ring adorns my finger to this day. She knew more about gold that I did. There is much to learn about faith. There are some strange mixtures around today but apply the acid test of Scripture to them and they are soon exposed as more alloy than gold; more psychology than scriptural faith.

Geologists are of the opinion that while there is plenty of gold left in the fields now being worked, major new gold strikes are unlikely in the future – so goodbye dreams of leading another gold rush to some new Klondike. It is safe to say that demand will always oustrip supply. That is why gold is such a good investment. It is also certain that people of faith will always be in demand because in this unbelieving world they are likely to remain a very special minority. The book of Job is the oldest book in the Bible and it deals with the oldest subject, suffering – what a book and what a man! The heat of the furnace in which Job found himself was intense but from the midst of the fire he could still say: 'When he has tried me, I shall come forth as gold' (Job 23:10). In 1520 Martin Luther wrote: 'The more Christian a man is, the more evils, sufferings, and deaths he must endure.' Is that the reason why the church in the west has faced so little suffering and persecution in the last century – because we are not really very Christian? It is widely accepted that the church at Laodicea is a picture of today's church: lukewarm, apathetic, indifferent, and lacking in zeal.

Martin Luther designed his own coat of arms which became known as Luther's rose. He used it to express the main principles of his own faith, especially salvation and justification by faith. He said it was the symbol of his theology. The centre is a black cross in the middle of a red heart, and the whole is surrounded by a white rose on a blue background, surrounded by a gold ring. He described the essence of what it portrayed in a letter he wrote to Spengler, the Clerk of Nuremburg.

'The first must be a cross, black in the heart, so that I remind myself that faith in the Crucified One saves me. For if we believe in our hearts, we are justified. Even though it is a black cross and mortifies and hurts, yet it leaves the heart in its natural colour (red). It does not destroy our natural personality. It does not kill, but it rather allows us to live. For the just LIVES by faith. This heart must be set in the midst of a white, gay rose, in order to show that faith produces happiness, comfort, and peace, and not as the world gives. For this reason the rose must be white and not red. For white is the colour of the spirits and all angels. This rose is set in the centre of an azure background in order to show that this joy is the beginning of a future heavenly joy. And this background is set in a golden ring in order to show that this blessedness in heaven is everlasting and will never end, and is more precious than all joy and earthly possessions, just as gold is the most precious of all metals.'

Billy Graham says: 'I am convinced that the current popularity of evangelical Christianity in America will be short-lived.' He attributes this to 'secular materialism which is eating away at the vitals of the country.' In Britain, the persecution is more likely to come as a result of conflict with the religions which immigrants have brought into the nation – especially the Muslims who are intent on bringing Britain under the sway of Mohammedanism. Other factors which will undoubtedly arouse bitter opposition against Christians who are loyal to the teachings of Scripture will be the increasing militancy of gays and lesbians. However, suffering is not a mark of God's disapproval but rather of his approval and confidence in the church. When Peter and the rest of the apostles had been beaten and threatened by the Jerusalem council they 'rejoiced that they were counted worthy to suffer shame for the name of Jesus' (Acts 5:41).

One of the most moving sights in Rome today is the great ruin of the Colosseum where so many Christians suffered martyrdom in the days of the early church. The deaths of the mostly unknown believers became the sport for the mocking, jeering crowds on Roman holidays. Blood flowed in rivers as men, women and children were thrown to the lions and tigers in the arena, while others were crucified or coated with pitch and used as living torches. There did not seem to be any hope of the infant church surviving such a holocaust. But today in the centre of the arena what do we find but a cross with the inscription: 'Hail to thee, O Cross, the only hope!'

The blood of the martyrs over and over again has proved to be the seed of the church. It has proved to be the case in this century in Uganda, in Korea, in China, and in many other countries where today Christianity is flourishing as never before. Only eternity will reveal just how many thousands upon thousands have sealed their testimony with their blood, especially in the Third World. The result is that the centre of the Christian missionary activity is shifting from the West to the Third World. It is in these so-called poor countries that one finds churches of power with signs and wonders confirming the preaching of the gospel.

In Zaire following Independence in 1960, missionaries say that it has been impossible to count all the martyrs. Whole villages, some composed entirely of believers, were laid waste. Yet rebel leaders were forced to confess: 'The more we kill these Christians the more they multiply. They have a power we haven't got.' After things settled down, revival came to many parts of Zaire and the church emerged stronger than ever and continues to grow to this day.

In February 1965, the WEC Missionary Society held a special service of remembrance and prayer for the missionaries who had been martyred in Zaire following

Independence – there were thirty-two Protestant missionaries listed from several denominations. At the service, Len Moules mentioned the story of Muriel Harman, a Canadian WEC missionary who was martyred in 1964 after a great deal of suffering. He said, 'The Word of the Lord came to Muriel Harman early in the days of struggle and suffering. Its source was from her reading Philips' translation of 1 Peter 1:6: "This means tremendous joy to you, I know, even though at present you are temporarily harassed by all kinds of trials and temptations. *This is no accident* – it happens to prove your faith, which is infinitely more valuable than gold." Muriel encouraged her fellow missionaries who were beaten and flung upon a live ant-hill, and as almost naked she walked with her fellow missionaries in similar affliction. With the blood trickling on to her bare flesh from a head wound from rubber truncheons, she encouraged herself, "This is no accident." The text was her anchorage when driven into the death room to be machine-gunned down with many others.'

Len Moules shared that, at the height of the crisis, he was in the London Headquarters of WEC, when a veteran lady missionary with over forty-seven years of service came to see him. He was a little afraid of meeting her, feeling that the news might be too distressing for her. 'But I found a triumphant soul. On seeing me, she said, "Len, He is making up His number – Revelation 6:11! He is making up His number." I replied, "Amen," and hurried to the office to look up Revelation 6:11 to find out to what I had said Amen! This is what I read: "And white robes were given unto every one of them; and it was said unto them, that they should rest yet for a little season, until their fellowservants also and their brethren, that should be killed as they were, should be fulfilled." The completed task of worldwide evangelisation is at a scheduled cost of martyrs. The Scriptures say so. The full price has not yet been paid – otherwise Christ would have already returned.

The programme and the price are interlinked and inseparable.'

Suffering and faith are inseparable. If we would be rich in faith, then we are going to have to be willing to pay the price of suffering for Christ.

Chapter Eleven

Faith is for Ever

Faith is as eternal as God Himself. Although love is the greatest of the three abiding virtues it is not more lasting. Faith, hope, and love are as everlasting as the Godhead of Father, Son, and Holy Spirit. When Scripture speaks of faith, hope, and love abiding it means that they will endure throughout the endless ages of eternity.

Although the phrase 'the faith of God' (Romans 3:3) occurs only once in Scripture, nevertheless it opens up marvellous avenues of thought. The faith of God is a faith that never fails. It is a faith free from any doubt. It has not failed, it will not fail, it cannot fail.

Venturing out on the promises of God is not pushing a trembling toe out onto a slack wire high above a circus ring of chance. Rather it is stepping boldly out on a highway of concrete a mile thick. When God wanted to reassure Abraham we read: 'Because God could swear by no greater he swore by himself' (Hebrews 6:13). It has been said many times, it was a good thing that God did not swear by heaven and earth because one day even they will pass away. Equally, it was well that God did not affirm His oath by some archangel, for such beings have fallen. But there is no one greater than God.

Fulfilled prophecy is a miracle in the highest realm of all – the mind. It is proof that God is God, evidence that He has absolute faith in all He has done and said, because He is God only-wise and all-wise. He knows what he is doing and invites us to trust Him forever. Faith believes and accepts that all unfulfilled prophecy will certainly be fulfilled in God's time and way.

Faith works by love (Galatians 5:6). God's faith is never separated from His love. God believes in everything He does – because He does everything in love and He never does anything He does not believe in. Every word He has spoken will stand; and He stands by every word He has spoken. The Scripture cannot be broken; it is one of the few unbreakable things in this world. God's word is forever settled in heaven.

Eternity is that state of pefect faith in God for ever. Our faith is that we shall be with Christ – 'that where I am there you may be also' (John 14:3). And we shall be like Him – 'for we shall see him as he is' (1 John 3:2). Everything stems from Calvary. The cross is the centre of everything, not only in time but in eternity. That is why faith does not attempt to explain away the hard things but is content to hold the mystery of the faith in a pure conscience. Faith does not need to know everything now, nor does it have to have it all explained now. Faith rests content in the knowledge that God knows everything and in His time He will reveal all.

From time to time God allows us to experience a sample of His omniscience by a manifestation of the word of knowledge. When it happens it is wonderful and creates faith. It is thrilling to see more and more convincing manifestations of this precious gift of the Spirit which often solves in moments what otherwise may take weeks of counselling. It is all a matter of moving in faith and obedience at all times. When I was pastoring in Bishop Auckland in County Durham, a lady called Ruby returned to the Lord who had been backslidden for many years. She visited her sister, Alma, who lived in the South of England, and Alma was so impressed with the peace which Ruby had that she too was stirred. Alma and Ruby had both let their faith lapse when they had left home in their younger days. Alma had drifted into spiritualism and had gained some status in those circles, practising clairaudience and clairvoyance with leading spiritists. Yet she was a member of her local parish church council and saw nothing inconsistent in this.

Eventually, Alma visited her sister Ruby in Bishop Auckland. Many of the old people in the church remembered her from her younger days and welcomed her. However, the day after her arrival I had a visit from my church secretary, Charles Brown. Alma had been round at their house the previous evening and they had closed their evening of happy fellowship together with a time of prayer. Charles told me: 'Pastor, you have got to do something. I tell you, Alma prayed, but it was "not her" – it was something else, and it was evil.' Charles was a wonderful Christian, a coal-pit deputy and so a man used to danger and not easily scared – but he was that morning. I promised to call and visit Alma that afternoon.

I had to call on a bereaved person and was delayed in visiting Alma, and had only a short time to spend with her. In fact I virtually said only two things to her: 'Remember, so far as we know, Judas never called Jesus Lord; he called him Master, but never Lord. And no matter what has happened in our lives the Lord can restore the years which the locust has eaten.' With that I left, feeling very inadequate. But God had put the words in my mouth.

Unbeknown to me before I had called on her, Alma had decided that she wanted to finish with spiritism. However, she was still not convinced that her spirit guides were evil. One of her familiar spirits had appeared to her and she had said to it: 'Jesus is my Master.' Without more ado he had bowed and said: 'Jesus is my Master too.' After I had left her she began to look up the Scripture I had quoted about locusts in Joel 2:25. She got hold of a concordance and looked up others where locusts were mentioned. In Revelation 9:3 she read about the unloosing of the great locust army on the earth, and what struck her was verse 8 where it said 'they had hair as the hair of women.' All her familiar spirits had long hair like women. She began to realise their true nature as evil. When her strongest spirit guide appeared to her after this she challenged him afresh and said, 'Jesus is my Lord.' The result was totally different than before. Now, she said, he became very angry and told her that she must never say that again and he left her – never to return. She was set free and joined in our prayer meeting at the church with great joy and freedom. She was delivered and made whole and the means was what can only be termed a word of knowledge given by the Holy Spirit.

I am sure that I could have spent hours and hours arguing and seeking to convince her without getting anywhere, but two sentences spoken in the Holy Spirit made the difference. It is this realm the Holy Spirit is bringing the church into – the realm of the supernatural, the realm of faith and power.

There are not many things we can take out of this world with us – but faith is one of them. We came into this world naked and go out the same. There is no doubt that our faith and our love will largely determine our place in Christ's kingdom. Faith and love will prove to be the only access cards to the true riches when we are received into those everlasting habitations (Luke 16:9-11).

There will be no souls to save in that day, no sick ones to heal, no demon-possessed to deliver, no bereaved ones to comfort, but there will be cities to rule and an ever-expanding universe to fill with the praises and glory of God. God is infinite, therefore we His creatures will always find that there is the need for trust as He leads us through glorious age after glorious age.

When we see this, then every day becomes a challenge for our faith to increase as we recognise that our heavenly Father is planning our lives and giving us more and more opportunities to exercise our faith. Every need is a chance to give and thereby increase our faith. Every sick person is a challenge to believe for His healing power. Always we should be endeavouring to build up an atmosphere of faith and love in our hearts, in our homes, in our churches.

Thousands of churches every year report no conversions but that is not the norm-it is the abnormal due to one thing and one thing alone: unbelief. Thousands more never see anyone miraculously healed but let one person of real faith come along and things begin to happen.

At the Minehead Celebration and Conference of Assemblies of God in May 1985, in an endeavour to bring a greater sense of togetherness among the thousands who gather for this event, we hired a vast circus-type tent. One of our guest speakers was Benson Idahosa from Nigeria. Throughout the week the atmosphere of faith continued to rise – in spite of more than a few problems which are always associated with tents of that size. Benson's ministry was particularly blessed although others also preached with great power and acceptance. It is a fact that when the word of God is preached under the anointing of the Holy Spirit and with assurance then faith is ministered to the hearers.

On the Friday evening I was on the platform with other leaders and ministers. After Benson had finished preaching he made an appeal and many responded. Some came out for salvation, others for reconsecration, and a great number made their way to the front for healing. Along with other leaders I came down from the platform and began praying with the many sick ones. Ministers and counsellors were praying everywhere and many wonderful things happened that night, including members of the camp staff responding to Christ. Just as we were finishing praying a lady came through with a friend in an electrically driven wheelchair. The lady explained that she had been unable to get through to the front before this owing to the crowds and the difficulty of getting the wheelchair moving over the grass and uneven floor, only parts of which were covered with matting. I was with my friend and colleague, Veyne Austin of Dartford. When I saw this sad case in the wheelchair my first instinct was to turn around to the platform and call for Benson Idahosa to come and minister to her. To my chagrin I found that he had left the platform – leaving us with this difficult case – and I must confess that I was not pleased with friend Idahosa at that moment. So much for my faith!

However, Veyne and I talked to her and ministered to her, laying our hands upon her in the name of the Lord Jesus and praying for her healing. The friend who was helping with the wheelchair was one who had befriended her during the week and they had tried to help each other, for both had problems. The lady in the wheelchair was a Welsh lady called Mrs Ivy Craven from Cwmbran. As she was pushed to the front she found everyone praying for her with compassion so that it seemed to her that she was coming through a tunnel of prayer as many stretched out their hands towards her in love. There really was a tremendous sense of the Lord's presence in the tent that night. After Veyne and I had prayed for Ivy Craven without a sign that anything had happened, we turned and prayed with one or two more. A minute or two later I turned around to see Ivy Craven up on the platform, out of her wheelchair and walking. I learned that after we had left Ivy, a lady from Veyne Austin's church encouraged her to stand up out of her wheelchair. At first her legs buckled then straightened and in a matter of moments she was walking. Her two young sons were with her, watching in wonderment. I asked one of them whether he had ever seen his mother stand up unaided before, and he told me that he had not.

Ivy Craven had been ill for ten years and confined to a wheelchair for five years. What a thrill it was the next morning to see her leaving Butlin's Camp at Minehead pushing her wheelchair, and waving excitedly to everyone. Her pastor, Les Thomas, of Cwmbran, in a report he sent me as editor of *Redemption Tidings*, said: 'As her pastor, I had never seen Ivy stand up and had no idea how tall she was. She can now walk and run and it is incredible to see her dive into the pool on our weekly swim with the church folk. She has not sat in her wheelchair since and gives God the glory for her wonderful healing and new life. Her testimony has affected many people in the area and her energy seems endless.'

Ivy was at our Minehead conference the following year in 1986 confirming that her healing was lasting. Before writing this story (April 1987) I checked again with her pastor and he confirmed the lastingness of this wonderful miracle. Because of the way this happened, no-one but the Lord received the glory but the Lord graciously allowed many of us to share in it to the encouragement of our faith.

Smith Wigglesworth was so right when he declared: 'You will never get anywhere except you are in continual pursuit of all the power of God'. There is no discharge in this war; no standing still in this race. All the people of faith I know are pressing toward the mark for the high calling of God as hard as they know how. The men and women of faith are also more excited than I can ever recollect before in my lifetime. There is a sense of divine expectancy in the air. Faith is on a tip-toe of readiness waiting for God to visit His people in power.

Let us never forget that Christ is the Author and Perfecter of faith. From all eternity, before the incarnation, before the creation of the universe, there never was a moment when the Son did not perfectly trust the Father. 'On the cross he brought faith to its highest conceivable development, and so became its Perfecter' (Hebrews 12:2) – G.H. Lang. Christ is at the heart of divine revelation and the cross is at the centre of all God's dealings. Faith can safely grow and grow as long as it focuses on the Lamb of God and is anchored in His Calvary. But faith adrift from Christ and the Cross is a dangerous maverick. The cross is timeless; it is the baring of the very heart of God. It is here that true faith makes its home and refuses to stray from it one iota.

Bibliography

Introduction

African Plenty by Fred Ramsbottom (Marshall-Pickering 1987).

Chapter 1 Faith Starts Here

'Exodus' by J.C. Connell, in *New Bible Commentary*, (IVF 1954 edition).

The Knowledge of the Holy by A.W. Tozer (James Clarke & Co. Ltd 1965).

Chapter 2 Saving Faith

Wesley's Journal, 7th Feb 1736, Feb and May 1738. (Abridged version: Percy L. Parker, Isbister & Co Ltd 1902).

What the Bible Teaches by R.A. Torrey (Oliphants Ltd, 1957 edition).

Chapter 3 Faith in the Saviour

The Master Theme of the Bible by J. Sidlow Baxter (Coverdale House Publishers Ltd., London 1973).

The Holiest of All by Andrew Murray (Nisbet & Co Ltd, London 1934).

Christ and the Scriptures by Adolph Saphir (Morgan & Scott Ltd, London).

Christ in All the Scriptures by A.M. Hodgkin (Pickering & Inglis Ltd, 1922).

Thousand Acts and Facts by Hy. Pickering (Pickering & Inglis Ltd, London).

Chapter 4 Faith and the Holy Spirit

The Happiest People on Earth by Demos Shakarian (Hodder & Stoughton 1975).

And Signs Followed – The Story of Charles S. Price (Autobiography) (Logos International, Plainfield, New Jersey 07060). (Available from Valley Books of Monmouth).

Westminster Record, September 1964, Dr. D. Martyn Lloyd-Jones.

Joy Unspeakable by Dr. D. Martyn Lloyd-Jones (Kingsway 1984).

My Personal Testimony to Pentecost by William Booth-Clibbon (Assemblies of God in Gt. Britain & Ireland 1929).

Twelve Baskets Full (Volume 1) by Watchman Nee (Church Book Room, Hong Kong 1966).

Chapter 5 Feed Your Faith

How to Obtain Fulness of Power by R.A. Torrey (Oliphants Ltd 1955).

Christ and the Scriptures by Adolph Saphir (Morgan & Scott Ltd).

The Craft of The Sermon by W.E. Sangster (Epworth Press, London 1954). Re-issued by Marshall Pickering 1985. ISBN 0-7208-0404-4.

How to Master the English Bible by James M. Gray, D.D. (Bible Institute, Chicago, 1904).

Chapter 6 Faith to Give

One Thousand Acts and Facts by Hy. Pickering (Pickering & Inglis Ltd).

Chapter 7 Soul-Winning Faith

Evangelism by James A. Stewart (Revival Literature, Chattanooga, USA).

Redemption Tidings, Vol 59 No. 35 (1st Sept. 1983) (Assemblies of God in Great Britain & Ireland).

Chapter 8: Faith for the Miraculous

The John G. Lake Sermons, edited by Gordon Lindsay (Christ for the Nations, Inc. P.O. Box 769000, Dallas, Texas 753-9000 USA).

When God Makes a Pastor by W.F.P. Burton (Victory Press, London SW4, 1934).
A Doctor Heals by Faith by Christopher Woodward. (Max Parrish, London 1953).
The Independent, 10 March 1987.
Redemption, March 1987 (Interview of Anne Watson by Brian Hewitt) (Assemblies of God in Great Britain & Ireland).

Chapter 9 The Language of Faith

Plundering Hell by Ron Steele (The Story of Reinhard Bonnke) (Marshalls 1984).
Prayer: Key to Revival by Dr. Paul Yonggi Cho (Word UK Ltd 1984).
Lewi Pethrus: A Spiritual Memoir (Logos International, Plainfield, New Jersey 1973). Available from Valley Books of Monmouth, U.K.

Chapter 10 Faith in the Furnace of Suffering

The Bible, translation by James Moffatt (Hodder & Stoughton Ltd., London 1934).
In the Arena of Faith by Eric Sauer (Paternoster Press, London 1955).
Till Armageddon by Billy Graham (Grason, Minneapolis, USA 1981).
This Is No Accident, edited by Leonard C.J. Moules (WEC, London SE19).

Bible quotations are from the King James Authorised Version.